ST. MATTHEW'S EARTHQUAKE

Also by Paul Hinnebusch:

Jesus, the New Elijah
Praise, a Way of Life

St. Matthew's Earthquake

*Judgment and Discipleship
in the Gospel of Matthew*

Paul Hinnebusch, O.P.

SERVANT BOOKS
Ann Arbor, Michigan

Cover photo courtesy of the University of California, Berkeley
Book design by John B. Leidy

Published by Servant Books
     P.O. Box 8617
     Ann Arbor, Michigan 48107

Printed in the United States of America
ISBN 0-89283-093-X

Contents

Acknowledgments

The idea for this book came to me from a sentence written by John L. McKenzie in *The Jerome Biblical Commentary*. Commenting on Mt 21:10, "the whole city was stirred," Father McKenzie writes, "*Stirred*: lit., 'shaken,' the word that would be used to describe an earthquake" (JBC 43:143). Then I discovered another sentence in the same commentary, regarding Mt 8:23-27: "Mark's 'whirlwind' has become a *seismos*, 'earthquake,' a cosmic disturbance" (JBC 43:59).

My inspiration developed when I read John P. Meier, "The Signs at Jesus' Death," *The Vision of Matthew* (New York: The Paulist Press, 1978), pp. 33-35.

The second chapter, The "Earthquake at Sea," was enriched by O. Lamar Cope, "The Stilling of the Storm," *Matthew, A Scribe Trained for the Kingdom of God* (Washington: The Catholic Biblical Quarterly Monograph Series 5, 1976), pp. 96-99.

Gerhard Von Rad, *Old Testament Theology*, Vol. II (New York: Harper and Row), pp. 282-286, was especially valuable in writing my fourteenth chapter, "Glory and Victory in the House of God."

Parts of my fifteenth chapter, "Innocent Blood Betrayed," were inspired by Albert Vanhoye, *Structure and Theology of the Accounts of the Passion in the Synoptic Gospels* (Collegeville: The Liturgical Press, 1967), p. 16.

Since my ideas for this book have developed over a period of twenty years of Bible teaching, it is impossible to recall every source used. In many instances I have forgotten how these ideas first came to life, and my classroom notes give no indication of most of my sources. I apologize to anyone whom I may have overlooked in giving credits.

I thank the Very Reverend Richard T.A. Murphy, O.P., S.T.D., S.S.D., for reading the original manuscript and for suggesting certain revisions which I have made.

I am grateful to Mr. Bert Ghezzi of Servant Publications for discovering in my manuscript the primary importance of the theme of discipleship. I am grateful also to Miss Ann Spangler for editing the manuscript for publication and for the many improvements in literary style which she suggested.

I am indebted to the following sources for use of their translations of scripture. The symbols that follow indicate the versions used.

a — *The Anchor Bible*, copyright © 1966 by Doubleday and Company, Inc. All rights reserved.

b — The latest edition of *La Bible de Jerusalem*, 1973, Les Editions du Cerf.

c — *The Holy Bible*, copyright © 1962 by the Confraternity of Christian Doctrine.

d — Douay-Rheims.

e — *The New English Bible*, copyright © The Delegates of the Oxford University Press and the Syndics of the Cambridge University Press, 1961, 1970.

g — The Grail Psalter, copyright © 1963, by The Grail, England.

j — *The Jerusalem Bible*, copyright © 1966 by Darton, Longman & Todd Ltd and Doubleday & Company, Inc. All rights reserved.

k — King James Version.

m — *Modern Language Bible*, available in the *Layman's Parallel Bible*, copyright © 1969, Zondervan Publishing House.

n — *The New American Bible*, copyright © 1970 by the Confraternity of Christian Doctrine, Washington, D.C.

r — *Revised Standard Version*, copyright © 1946, 1952, 1971, Division of Christian Education of the National Council of the Churches of Christ in the United States of America.

INTRODUCTION

Four times in his gospel, Matthew speaks of an earthquake, and it is clear that he is speaking metaphorically.

First, as Jesus enters Jersualem on Palm Sunday, the city is shaken as if by an earthquake (Mt 21:10).

Secondly, in telling of the storm at sea, Matthew rewrites Mark's account of the storm. He replaces Mark's word "squall" (Mk 4:37) with "earthquake" (Mt 8:24). Why does he describe a squall on the Sea of Galilee with a word whose primary meaning is earthquake? Is he again using symbolic language as he does in the Palm Sunday account?

Thirdly, an earthquake occurs at the death of Jesus (Mt 27:52).

Fourthly, there is "a mighty earthquake" (28:2, n) at his resurrection. In these last two cases, is Matthew again using symbolic apocalyptic language?

Yet another reference to the earthquake exists in the story of the Magi. "Wise men came from the East to Jerusalem, saying, 'Where is he who has been born king of the Jews?' . . . When Herod the king heard this, he was troubled, and all Jerusalem with him" (Mt 2:2-3, r). The agitation of Herod and of the whole city prefigures the agitation of the city when Jesus enters it on Palm Sunday (Mt 21:10). Therefore it also prefigures the earthshaking event of the passion, death, and resurrection of the King of the Jews.

Following Jesus into the Earthquake

The story of the storm at sea in Matthew's version is introduced by a little passage concerning discipleship. Jesus is preparing to cross the sea (Mt 8:18) when a scribe offers to become his disciple. Jesus responds by speaking of the high cost of discipleship. He ends with the words, "*Follow me,* **and** leave the dead to bury their own dead" (Mt 8:22). Matthew then goes immediately into the story of the storm with the words, "And when he got into the boat, his disciples *followed him*" (Mt 8:23, r).

Matthew implies that Jesus deliberately invited his disciples into the storm at sea. "Follow me," he said. Leading them into the boat, he led them into the storm. Matthew describes this storm as an "earthquake," because it prefigures the earth-shaking event of the Lord's death and resurrection. Disciple-ship means following the Lord through his passion, death, and resurrection.

We shall examine in detail Matthew's five earthquake pas-sages to justify the above interpretation and to bring out the unity of Matthew's earthquake theme. The whole Christ-event is earthshaking. Our lives, too, will be shaken to their depths as we follow Jesus into the earthquake of his Paschal Mystery.

The Plan of the Book

Everything in this volume is presented in relationship with the deeper meaning of our Lord's coming into Jerusalem on the first Palm Sunday. Matthew presents this coming as an intro-duction to and interpretation of the death and resurrection of Jesus. "The very stone which the builders rejected has become the head of the corner" (Mt 21:42, r).

The first part of the book examines Matthew's earthquake imagery as "day of the Lord" symbolism borrowed from the Old Testament. We begin with the words, "As he entered the city, the whole city was shaken as if by an earthquake" (Mt 21:10). Here, the imagery of the earthquake forebodes judg-ment upon Jerusalem and its inhabitants because they refuse to be disciples of Jesus. But at the same time it presages the great day of the Lord, the death and resurrection of Jesus, in which he is given all authority in heaven and on earth, and sends his missionaries to make disciples of all the nations.

The second part of the book treats of "naked obedience," the dying of self which is necessary for following Jesus in whole-hearted love.

In the third section, the judgment theme comes forward

again in a vivid way. But along with it there resounds a message of hope for all the peoples of the earth, who are invited to become disciples.

Matthew's Tapestry

Matthew's gospel is like a tapestry woven from many threads to present a striking portrait of Jesus. In weaving, cloth is made on a loom by interlacing warp with woof. The warp is a series of yarns extended lengthwise on the loom. The woof is the filling thread or yarn. In Matthew's tapestry, the warp consists of threads from the Old Testament, certain salvation themes. These threads from the Old Testament run all through Matthew's gospel, forming a durable texture into which everything else is woven.

Upon this warp of Old Testament themes, Matthew weaves the woof, the words and deeds of Jesus. He interprets the life and sayings of Jesus in the light of these themes, so that the life of Jesus stands out with vivid new meaning.

Perhaps Matthew would have been surprised to know that I find some things in his gospel which he may not have been fully aware of himself. For I am sure that some critics will accuse me of reading into Matthew things that he did not intend to say. But there are great riches in the four gospels which the Holy Spirit intended to say, even though the evangelists may not always have been fully aware of all that the Spirit was saying through them.

In every book I have written, readers have found things that I was not fully conscious of saying. Indeed, this very volume illustrates that fact. I thought I was writing a book about Matthew's earthquake. But some of the first readers of the manuscript saw it primarily as a book on discipleship, and I too now see it that way.

Throughout the book I try to remain faithful to the solid principles of scriptural interpretation. As the fruit of my efforts, a spiritual meaning emerges, which I pray will bear fruit in the lives of you, the readers of this book.

I was repeatedly amazed at what was unfolding on my pages

as I wrote them. New light dawned for me as I tried to express the light I had already seen. May this same amazement rejoice the hearts of all who will be patient enough to follow my threads through the duller areas of my written tapestry.

Part I

St. Matthew's Earthquake

For Matthew, the whole Christ-event is
earthshaking. He presents it under the
metaphor of an earthquake, into which
we must all follow Jesus.

ONE

The Earthquake
As Jesus Enters Jerusalem

As Jesus advanced towards Jerusalem from the Mount of Olives on the first Palm Sunday, great crowds acclaimed him, shouting their hosannas. "As he entered Jerusalem the whole city was stirred to its depths, demanding, 'Who is this?'" (Mt 21:10, n). The Greek verb, *seio*, translated as "stirred to its depths," literally means "to rock," "to quake." The noun *seismos*, earthquake, comes from this verb. We could translate the passage: "As he entered Jerusalem the whole city was shaken as if by an earthquake, demanding, 'Who is this?'"

This is obviously metaphorical language. Quite likely it is a reference to the prophet Haggai:

> One moment yet, a little while, and I will shake the heavens and the earth, the sea and the dry land. I will shake all the nations, and the treasures of the nations will come in, and I will fill this house with glory, says the Lord of hosts (Hg 2:6-7, n).

Haggai speaks of the same temple (the house) that Jesus is about to enter and tells us in metaphorical language that the inauguration of the messianic era will be an earthshaking event. Jesus is entering Jerusalem and the temple precisely as Messiah: "Hosanna to the Son of David!" (Mt 21:9).

When Matthew says that Jerusalem was shaken as if by an earthquake as Jesus entered the city, he is proclaiming that "the age to come" has arrived! Jesus inaugurates the eschatological era by coming to assert his messianic authority in the temple. Thus the prophecy of Haggai is fulfilled: "I will fill this house with glory" (Hg 2:7).

Haggai twice employs this imagery of God shaking the heavens and the earth. First, God shakes the heavens and the earth, and all the treasures of the nations come flowing to Jerusalem to fill God's house with glory (Hg 2:6-9). Secondly, God shakes the heavens and the earth and overthrows the kingdoms of the earth that stand in opposition to him (Hg 2:21-22). The prophet continues, "On that day, says the Lord of hosts, I will take you, Zerubbabel, son of Shealtiel, my servant, says the Lord, and I will set you as a signet ring; for I have chosen you, says the Lord of hosts" (Hg 2:23, n).

The king's signet ring is a symbol of his authority. When he impresses it upon a decree, that decree is executed with power and authority. God calls Zerubbabel his signet ring because God will use him in power to carry out his earthshaking plans. Zerubbabel is the son of David, who should have been king in Jerusalem, but instead he is only a puppet of the King of Persia. In reality Haggai is speaking, not of Zerubbabel, but of the coming Messiah. When God carries out his plans through the Messiah, prefigured by Zerubbabel, the heavens and the earth will be shaken and kingdoms will be shattered.

Jesus is God's signet ring. He is the instrument God uses to execute his earthshaking plans for the nations. The kingdoms ranged against God and his Messiah are overthrown, and God's reign is established (see Ps 2).

"Who Is This?"

The story of the storm at sea (Mt 8:23-27) and the story of Jesus walking on the water (Mt 14:22-33) are as familiar to Christians as the story of Palm Sunday (Mt 21:1-11). But not everyone has noticed the close relationship existing among those stories as Matthew tells them. All of them are answering the great question, "Who is Jesus?" As Jesus enters Jerusalem on Palm Sunday, the whole city, shaken as if by an earthquake, demands, "Who is this?" The same question had been asked when Jesus calmed another "earthquake," the storm at sea: "What sort of man is this, that even the winds and the sea obey him?" (Mt 8:27, n).

The question is answered during yet another storm when Jesus and Peter walk towards each other on the waves: "Those in the boat worshipped him, saying, 'Truly, you are the Son of God!'" (Mt 14:33, r). And the same answer is given by the pagan centurion and the guards on Golgotha at the Lord's death: "When the centurion and those who were with him, keeping watch over Jesus, saw the earthquake and what took place, they were filled with awe, and said, 'Truly, this was the Son of God!'" (Mt 27:54, r).

Thus, in Matthew's literary plan, a relationship exists between the metaphorical earthquake that occurs as Jesus enters Jerusalem (21:10) and the earthquake that takes place at the death of Jesus (27:51). The question asked at the first quake, "Who is this?" is answered at the second, "Truly, this was the Son of God." Are the earthquakes at the death and resurrection of Jesus (27:51; 28:2) also metaphoric or symbolic like the previous one (21:10)? The same question must be asked concerning the "earthquake" which is the storm at sea.

The Real Earthquake

Jerusalem is shaken "as if" by an earthquake as Jesus enters. But Matthew will show that the real "earthquake"—the real earthshaking inauguration of the messianic kingdom—takes place at Jesus' death and resurrection. In Matthew's literary plan, the events of Jesus' entry into Jerusalem symbolically prefigure his death and resurrection; he is the rejected stone that becomes head of the corner. Thus the first "earthquake," the one at Jesus' entry into the city, holds the clue to the metaphorical meaning of the second, the one that took place at his death. Is Matthew using apocalyptic symbolism in speaking of these earthquakes? Let us examine the evidence.

Earthquake Imagery in the Prophets

The earthquakes that occurred at the Lord's death and resurrection recall the stereotyped imagery used by the prophets and the apocalyptic writers to speak of the day of the Lord. The day of the Lord was always a theophany, a time when God appeared in order to judge his enemies and rescue his people by establishing his reign. The prophets described these divine interventions as earthshaking. They spoke in terms of earthquakes and "skyquakes." The earth trembled, the heavenly bodies were troubled, the skies were darkened.

Amos, for example, spoke of the day of the Lord as a day in which God would intervene to restore justice and punish social injustice and oppression of the poor. In Amos's symbolic imagery, the earth trembles, rises up, tosses about, settles down again. The skies too are disturbed, the sun sets at noon, the whole earth is darkened (see Am 8:8-10). The whole creation is concerned about right order in human affairs. Repeatedly the prophets call all creation to witness against human injustice and sinfulness (see Mi 6:1-2; Is 1:2-4).

For Joel, the day of the Lord is a day of judgment upon the nations round about Jerusalem. That day Jerusalem is established in peace and salvation (Jl 4:11-21, n; 3:11-21, r). Again in this passage we have the imagery of earthquakes and the shaking of the heavens:

> For near is the day of the Lord
>   in the valley of decision.
> Sun and moon are darkened,
>   and the stars withhold their brightness.
> The Lord roars from Zion,
>   and from Jerusalem raises his voice;
> The heavens and the earth quake,
>   but the Lord is a refuge to his people,
>   a stronghold to the men of Israel.
>   (Jl 4:14-16, n; see also Jl 2:10; 3:3-4, n; 2:30-31, n)

For Zephaniah, too, the day of the Lord will be a "day of clouds and thick darkness" (Zep 1:15, r). Haggai, as we have seen, also uses the imagery of the shaking of the heavens and the earth.

The Great Day of the Lord

St. Matthew uses this same stereotyped imagery to describe the Lord's death and resurrection. Thus he expresses the truth that the death-resurrection of Jesus is the great day of the Lord. It is the day in which God triumphs over his enemies and inaugurates the eschatological era of his reign. In that day "the age to come" breaks definitively into the old era.

> Jesus cried again with a loud voice and yielded up his spirit. And behold, the curtain of the temple was torn in two, from top to bottom; and the earth shook, and the rocks were split; the tombs also were opened, and many bodies of the saints who had fallen asleep were raised, and coming out of the tombs after his resurrection they went into the holy city and appeared to many (Mt 27:50-53, r).

The earthquake at Jesus' death shatters the realm of the dead. The rocks are split, graves are thrown open, and the dead come forth. By dying, Jesus defeats death. Death must give up its captives. Freed from the underworld by the death of Jesus, the holy ones come forth from the tombs. They await the Lord's resurrection to enter with him into the holy city, the heavenly Jerusalem.

When the holy ones come forth from their tombs, it is a sign that the eschatological era foretold by the prophets has dawned: "Thy dead shall live, their bodies shall rise. O dwellers in the dust, awake and sing for joy!" (Is 26:19, r)

"And many of those who sleep in the dust of the earth shall awake, some to everlasting life, and some to shame and everlasting contempt." (Dn 12:2, r)

Matthew and Ezekiel's Dry Bones

Even more striking in reference to Matthew's description of the Lord's death is Ezekiel's vision of the resurrection of the dry bones. Ezekiel, too, speaks of an earthquake and the opening of tombs. In the Hebrew text of Ezekiel we read, "As I prophesied, there was a *noise*, and behold, a rattling; and the bones came together, bone to its bone" (Ez 37:7, r). But in the Septuagint, the Greek version, which may have influenced Matthew, the same verse reads, "As I prophesied, there was an earthquake *seismos*, and behold, a rattling. . . ."

A few verses later, Ezekiel says, "Thus says the Lord God: 'Behold, I will open your graves, O my people; and I will bring you home into the land of Israel. *And you shall know that I am the Lord*, when I open your graves, and raise you from your graves, O my people'" (Ez 37:12-13, r).

The pagan soldiers at the cross of Jesus "know the Lord" when they see the earthquake at the death of Jesus. They proclaim, "Truly, this was the Son of God!" (Mt 27:54, r). In the instant of his death, Jesus is manifested as Lord, for he splits open the graves, and the dead come forth.

"Earthquake," we said, symbolizes "day of the Lord." The death and resurrection of Jesus taken together make the one definitive day of the Lord. Matthew presents the death and resurrection as one apocalyptic event. He does this by using apocalyptic earthquake imagery to recount both events and by associating the resurrection of the holy ones with the death of Jesus. The death and resurrection of Jesus contains the resurrection of all of God's holy ones. Matthew symbolizes this strikingly by showing that the earthshaking event of the Lord's death breaks open the tombs, and the dead come forth. But they await the Lord's own resurrection before they enter into the holy city, the heavenly Jerusalem.

Two years after the prophecies of Amos, who spoke of the day of the Lord in earthquake imagery, a real earthquake occurred in Jerusalem (Am 1:1). No doubt this confirmed the word of the prophet and put the fear of God into the people. It must have been a memorable earthquake. Several centuries later Zechariah refers to it as he describes the coming of the Lord in apocalyptic imagery: "And the valley of the Lord's mountain . . . shall be filled up as it was filled up by the earthquake in the days of King Uzziah of Judah. Then the

Lord, my God, shall come, and all his holy ones with him" (Zec 14:5, n).

No doubt this text, too, influenced Matthew's description of the holy ones coming forth from their tombs at the moment of the Lord's death. His death and resurrection is truly the great day of the Lord—the day of his judgment upon the nations, and the victory of his holy ones.

TWO

"The Earthquake" at Sea

And when he got into the boat, his disciples followed him. And behold, there arose a great storm on the sea, so that the boat was being swamped by the waves; but he was asleep. And they went and woke him, saying, "Save us, Lord; we are perishing." And he said to them, "Why are you afraid, O men of little faith?" Then he rose and rebuked the winds and the sea; and there was a great calm (Mt 8:23-26).

Earlier, we asked the question: Why does Matthew describe the storm at sea with a word that means earthquake (Mt 8:24)? Is he using apocalyptic symbolism? Mark and Luke call the same storm *lailaps*, "squall" (Mk 4:37, n; Lk 8:23). Matthew substitutes *seismos* for *lailaps*. *Seismos* literally means "shaking," and especially, "earthquake." It can also mean "storm," a shaking of the air.

From Psalm 18, we gather that storms in Israel could be so violent that they were "skyshaking." Along with earthquakes, such storms became stock symbolic imagery for describing theophanies and days of the Lord. Psalm 18 describes such a theophany:

The earth swayed and quaked;
    the foundations of the mountains trembled . . .
And he inclined the heavens and came down,
    with dark clouds under his feet.

He mounted a cherub and flew,
　borne on the wings of the wind.
And he made darkness the cloak about him . . .
From the brightness of his presence
　coals were kindled to flame.
And the Lord thundered from heaven,
　the Most High gave forth his voice; . . .
He reached out from on high and grasped me;
　he drew me out of the deep waters.
　　　　　(Ps 18:8, 10-12, 13-14, 17, n)

Even though *lailaps*, "squall," adequately describes the kind of storm that rises suddenly on the Sea of Galilee, Matthew is not content with this word. By substituting *seismos*, he deliberately connects this storm to the earthquake *seismos* that occurs at the Lord's death and resurrection. The storm at sea and its calming by the Lord symbolize the Lord's passion and his victory over death in his resurrection. This will become clear later on.

When Matthew emphasizes that the disciples "followed him" into the boat (Mt 8:23), and therefore into the storm, he is assigning powerful meaning to the words, "Follow me," which occur in the immediately preceding verse (Mt 8:22). The disciples are to follow Jesus into his passion and resurrection, prefigured by the storm and its calming. Matthew tells his story to strengthen the "little faith" (Mt 8:26) of the first Christians as they endure the violent storms of persecution. Like the Lord's own passion and death, their share in his sufferings is "earthshaking." It betokens the new creation that is coming into being as the Lord's death and resurrection continue to take effect in his church.

The Cosmic Storm

By relating the storm at sea to the earthquake at the Lord's death and resurrection, Matthew presents the storm as an apocalyptic cosmic disturbance. He describes the storm in the same imagery used by the prophets to describe theophanies or manifestations of the Lord. And sure enough, in Matthew's account, the disciples address Jesus as "Lord." "Lord, save us!" (Mt 8:25, n). In Mark's and Luke's accounts of this event, he is merely called "Teacher" (Mk 4:38; Lk 8:24).

The Lord whom the disciples address is not merely Lord of nature, calming nature's storms. By using the apocalyptic word *seismos*, "earthquake," Matthew suggests a cosmic disturbance shaking heaven and earth. Thus he shows that Jesus masters not just nature's storms, but all the powers of evil and of death, and especially the satanic storms of persecution of the church.

Matthew says that Jesus "arose and rebuked the winds and the sea, and there was a great calm" (Mt 8:26, r). The word "rebuked" (*epitimam*) is used in the Greek Old Testament to express God's rebuke of his enemies: For you upheld my right hand and my cause, seated on your throne, judging justly. You rebuked the nations and destroyed the wicked; their name you blotted out forever and ever" (Ps 9:5-6, n).

The sea, in the Old Testament, represents the peoples who resist God's kingly rule: "Ah! the roaring of many peoples that roar like the roar of the seas! The surging of nations that surge like the surging of mighty waves! But God shall rebuke them, and they shall flee far away" (Is 17:12-13, n).

God rebukes the watery chaos when he creates the world. "Above the mountains the waters stood; at your rebuke they fled" (Ps 104:6-7, n). He rebukes the Red Sea when he delivers his people Israel. "He rebuked the Red Sea, and it was dried up" (Ps 106:9, n). God shall rebuke and master the wicked peoples and the forces of evil just as he mastered the primeval chaos when he created the world (Gn 1:2, 6). Genesis borrows imagery from ancient mythology to present God's work of creation and of deliverance in terms of the conquest of the sea and of Rahab, the sea monster: "You rule over the surging of the sea, you still the swelling of its waves. You have crushed Rahab with a mortal blow, with your strong arm you have scattered your enemies" (Ps 89:10, n). Rahab is a poetic personification symbolizing all rebellious creatures.

Such is the Old Testament background necessary for understanding our Lord's calming of the storm. Jesus rebukes the winds and the sea and is manifested as the one who establishes God's kingly rule over the rebellious peoples of the earth, and over the rebellious forces of evil throughout creation. When the Evangelists speak of Jesus' power over the stormy sea, they employ the same terminology that they use when referring to his power to expel evil spirits:

> But Jesus *rebuked* him, saying, *"Be silent,* and come out of him!" And the unclean spirit, convulsing him and crying out with a loud voice, came out of him (Mk 1:25-26, r).

> And he awoke and *rebuked* the wind, and said to the sea, "Peace! *Be still!"* And the wind ceased, and there was a great calm (Mk 4:39, r).

When Jesus stilled the sea, he performed no mere nature miracle, for the roaring sea symbolizes the rebellious nations and all the forces of evil. Jesus' power over the winds and the waves symbolizes his lordship over all the powers of evil, whether they be demons or human beings or the evil effects of sin upon nature itself.

By connecting the "earthquake" at sea to the earthquake at the Lord's death and resurrection, Matthew shows that Jesus achieves this lordship over the cosmic powers of evil by his death and resurrection. "He arose and rebuked the winds" (Mt 8:26). "Arose" (*egeiro*) is the same word used to speak of the Lord's resurrection (Mk 16:6). By the power of his death and resurrection, Jesus rebukes all the forces of evil and renders them powerless, thus establishing God's kingly rule.

The exorcisms performed by Jesus are also presented in relationship with his resurrection:

> "He rebuked the unclean spirit, saying to it, 'You dumb and deaf spirit, I command you, come out of him, and never enter him again.' . . . It came out, and the boy was like a *corpse.* . . . But Jesus took him by the hand and *raised him up* [*egeiro*], and he arose" (Mk 9:25-27).

The boy's exorcism symbolizes resurrection from death. The miracle occurs in the context of the Lord's prediction of his own death and resurrection (Mk 8:31, 35-37; 9:9).

Lord over Suffering and Death

If we understand the *seismos* on the Sea of Galilee in relation to the *seismos* at Jesus' death and resurrection, we will see that Jesus is not merely Lord of the winds and the sea. He is Lord of the waters of affliction, the overwhelming waters which in the Old Testament are a symbol of suffering and death. "Save me, O God, for the waters threaten my life . . . the flood overwhelms me" (Ps 69:2-3, n). "The breakers of death surged round about me, the destroying floods overwhelmed me" (Ps 18:5, n). Jesus reigns over suffering and death. The waters of the stormy sea foreshadow his own passion and death. He who calms the waves on the Sea of Galilee masters not only his personal suffering and death, but that of his disciples who follow him into the storm of persecution or into any kind of tribulation.

"'Follow me? . . .' And when he got into the boat, his disciples followed him" (Mt 8:22-23, r). Follow me through the storm at sea, through the cosmic earthquake, through the earthshaking events of my death and resurrection. Share in these by suffering persecution for my sake. Jesus addressed his words, "Why are you fearful, O you of little faith?" (Mt 8:26, c), not only to the disciples who were in the boat with him, but to every disciple who suffers persecution. The words are fully relevant to us today, for we can expect to follow the Lord through the storms raised up by the forces of evil in our times.

"Lord, Save Us!"

In Matthew's storm scene, the words, "Lord, save us!" are a prayer (8:25, n). In Mark and Luke, the disciples do not address Jesus in prayer. For them, Jesus is still only a teacher. They wake him in the storm-tossed boat, saying, "Teacher, do you not care if we perish?" (Mk 4:38, r). Wake up! Give us a hand! Grab an oar! Or better, pray to your God! Matthew tells the story in a way that is obviously patterned on the story of the storm at sea in the Book of Jonah. There the captain of the ship chides Jonah for sleeping peacefully while the ship perishes. "What are you doing asleep? Rise up, call upon your God! Perhaps God will be mindful of us so that we may not perish" (Jon 1:6, n).

In Psalm 18, the afflicted person describes his intense sufferings at the hands of his enemies in terms of stormy waters. "The breakers of death surged round about me, the destroying floods overwhelmed me" (Ps 18:5, n). He cries out to God, and the Lord responds with a theophany, described by the psalmist in storm and earthquake imagery. "The earth swayed and quaked. . . . He mounted a cherub and flew, borne on the wings of the wind. . . . He reached out from on high and grasped me; he drew me out of the deep waters. He rescued me from my mighty enemy . . . he rescued me, because he loves me" (Ps 18:8, 17, 20, n).

In another stormy scene on the Sea of Galilee, Peter steps out of the boat to walk on the water. Frightened by the violent wind, he begins to sink. In the instant that Peter cries out, "Lord, save me," Jesus reaches out and grasps him (Mt 14:30-31). "He reached out from on high and grasped me; he drew me out of the deep waters" (Ps 18:17, r). Once again, as in the first storm on the Sea of Galilee, Jesus says, "O man of little faith, why did you doubt?" (Mt 14:31, r).

When Jesus calms the sea, the dumbfounded disciples ask, "What sort of man is this that even the winds and sea obey him?" (Mt 8:27, n). The full answer to the question is given in Matthew's story of the other *seismos*, the earthquake at the Lord's death. When they saw the earthquake, the centurion and the others who were guarding Jesus said, "Truly, this was the Son of God!" (Mt 27:54, r).

"I Am With You Always"

Matthew's gospel is an ecclesial gospel, written to be read in the ecclesial assembly, the gathering of the church to celebrate the liturgy. The entire gospel consists of an inclusion between two references to God's presence with his church in the person of Jesus: "'His name shall be called Emmanuel' (which means God-with-us)" and "Lo, I am with you always, to the close of the age" (Mt 1:23; 28:20, r).

Matthew writes his gospel in a way that makes the Christian community contemporary with the earthly Jesus. The words and deeds of Jesus become actual and alive when Matthew's gospel is read. Matthew expects his readers or hearers to respond to the Lord, who is "with you always." Thus, he tells the life of Jesus as it is now being lived in the church. He tells it in such a way that the church already participates in this life, living it with Jesus, responding to his abiding presence in the fullness of faith, or rather, with a faith that is not yet as perfect as it should be. "Why are you afraid, O men of little faith?" (Mt 8:26, r).

Thus Matthew does not simply record the original storm on the Sea of Galilee when Jesus calmed the squall. He tells the story of the church undergoing the storms of persecution and whatever else it has to suffer from the forces of evil and death, but with Emmanuel still in her midst. Emmanuel has already mastered the storm of his own passion and death and has declared, "All authority in heaven and on earth has been given to me. . . . And lo, I am with you always" (Mt 28:18-20, r).

This is the One whom the disciples in the boat address as Lord: "Lord, save us!" For they represent the disciples of the whole era of the church, living the life of Jesus.

THREE

Follow Me!

Our understanding of Matthew's version of the storm at sea will be further enriched if we look at its immediate context. Jesus had been preparing to cross the Sea of Galilee. "He gave orders to go over to the other side" (Mt 8:18, r). Quite probably, in Matthew's ecclesial gospel, "the other side" symbolizes eternity, reached only through the storms of life, by following Jesus through his death and resurrection.

But before he could get into the boat, a scribe came up to him and declared, "Teacher, I will follow you wherever you go." And Jesus said to him, "Foxes have holes, and birds of the air have nests, but the Son of Man has nowhere to lay his head" (Mt 8:19-20, r).

"Another of the disciples said to him, 'Lord, let me first go and bury my father.' But Jesus said to him, 'Follow me, and leave the dead to bury their own dead'" (Mt 8:21-22, r).

Thus, before getting into the boat, Jesus teaches two lessons concerning the radical claim of discipleship and the cost of following him.

"And when he got into the boat, his disciples followed him" (8:23, r). The meaning of "follow" is clear from the two immediately preceding lessons. Leaving everything, they followed him into the storm at sea, into the storms raised up by the powers of evil. Jesus calms the storm, and in amazement the disciples say, "What sort of man is this, that even winds and sea obey him?" (8:27, n). Who is this man, who not only calms nature's storms, but masters the cosmic powers of evil? Who is this who dares to say: Strip yourselves of everything, follow me, and master the storm with my help?

Only the Lord of all could issue such a command and expect obedience. Knowing "what sort of man this is," Matthew tells the story in the light of the Lord's mastery of death in the resurrection. He is the Lord, to whom all power in heaven and on earth has been given (Mt 28:18). And so the disciples in Matthew's version call him "Lord," and not just "Teacher," as in Mark and Luke. If even the wind and the sea obey him, should we not obey him and become his disciples? "The Son of Man has no place to lay his head. . . . Follow me!" (8:20, 22, r). A disciple must be stripped of everything to follow Jesus into the storm.

The Lord

No ordinary teacher, but only the One who is called "Lord," has the authority to make such radical demands on another human being. A disciple follows an ordinary teacher and learns from him. But Jesus is infinitely more than a teacher. Matthew has just told us that "the crowds were astonished at his teaching, for he taught them as one who had authority, and not as their scribes" (7:29, r). Yet in nearly every incident immediately following these words, Jesus is addressed, not as teacher, but as Lord (*Kyrie*). This fact sets the stage for the story of the storm at sea, in which Jesus is indeed manifested as having the power of the *Kyrios*, the Lord.

"*Lord*, if you will, you can make me clean!" says the leper (8:2, r). "*Lord*, my servant is lying paralyzed at home, in terrible distress," says the centurion (8:6, r). "*Lord*, I am not worthy to have you come under my roof," he adds (8:8, r). "*Lord*, let me first go and bury my father," says the disciple (8:21, r).

Translations of Matthew that render *Kyrie* as "Sir" rather than "Lord" are mistaken. *Kyrie* does indeed mean "Sir." But if Matthew intended to have such a weak meaning he would hardly have taken pains to add it to the text. And it is clear that he did add it, since the title *Kyrie* is missing from the parallel passages in Mark and Luke. In those gospels no title of address is used by the leper, the scribe, or the disciple (Mk 1:40; Lk 9:57, 59). By contrast, Matthew writes his gospel in such a way that he will draw a profession of post-resurrection faith from his readers. The Jesus he presents is the Lord, endowed with all power in heaven and on earth. Matthew is thinking of this universal power, not only over the storms of nature, but over sin and death, when he writes that the disciples in the storm cry out, "Lord, save us!" (8:25, n). In Mark's and Luke's storm, we said, the disciples merely call him "Teacher," and do not pray to him to save them. Obviously, Matthew is rewriting Mark and Luke in a creative way, so that the church can respond to Jesus in the storms of evil and persecution.

Committed Discipleship

Discipleship is the theme of the entire section that ends with the storm. To follow Jesus as Lord, even into the storm, requires a deeper and more radical trust than simply to follow him as teacher. The Christian disciple not only opens his mind to the words of Jesus; he surrenders his whole life to the Person of Jesus as Lord.

Throughout Matthew's gospel, every committed disciple addresses Jesus as Lord. It is only the uncommitted who call him merely "Teacher." Such is the scribe in Mt 8:19, who is not yet able to commit himself to Jesus *Kyrios*, and therefore cannot accept the Lord's radical call to poverty: "The Son of Man has nowhere to lay his head" (8:20, n). Such too is the rich young man who "went away sad" (19:22, n) because he refused the challenge to commit his whole life and being to the Lord (19:21). He too addressed Jesus only as "Teacher" (19:16, n). And, finally, there is Judas, who reneged on his commitment to Jesus and addressed him merely as "Teacher" when he gave him the kiss of betrayal (Mt 26:49, n). He had lost whatever faith he possessed.

Though Matthew emphasizes that Jesus is a teacher, and one with authority, it is precisely because of that authority that, in Matthew, the true disciples address Jesus only as "Lord."

"Make Disciples"

Jesus shares this teaching authority with his disciples when he says to them, "All authority in heaven and on earth has been given to me. Go therefore and make disciples of all nations . . . teaching them to observe all that I have commanded you" (Mt 28:18-20, r).

"Make disciples," that is, show others how to commit their whole life and person to me. When they have yielded themselves to me as Lord, then they will be lovingly receptive and obedient as you teach them to observe all that I have commanded you. They will express their loving commitment to me by obeying my moral teaching.

When all the nations have been made into disciples, Haggai's "earthquake" prophecy will be fulfilled. The treasures of all the nations will be brought to the Lord's temple as votive offerings, for the nations will accept Jesus:

> For thus says the Lord of hosts:
>> One moment yet, a little while,
>>> and I will shake the heavens and the earth,
>>> the sea and the dry land.
>> I will shake all the nations,
>>> and the treasures of all the nations will come in,
>> And I will fill this house with glory,
>>> says the Lord of hosts.
>>>> (Hg 2:6-7, n)

This is the prophecy that Matthew seems to have in mind when he tells us that Jerusalem was shaken as if by an earthquake when Jesus came to the temple on Palm Sunday (Mt 21:10). The power of the earthshaking death and resurrection of the Lord has drawn the nations into discipleship. "In his name will the Gentiles hope" (Mt 12:21, r). The drawing power of the Lord's death and resurrection is mediated to all the nations through the disciples' endurance of the storms of persecution with the Lord.

In spite of the fury of the storms, which we will surely face, Jesus says to all of his disciples, as he steps into the boat,

(8:26), and if even Peter was a "man of little faith" (14:31), is there not hope for all of us, that we too will pass from "little faith" to the fullness of faith which will persevere till the end?

The storm at sea symbolizes the raging waters of temptation, tribulation, persecution, and eschatological testing, to which Christians sometimes succumb, denying the Lord. Jesus reaches out his hand to rescue Peter from sinking into the waters and, in so doing, symbolizes Peter's resurrection with Jesus after his triple denial of him. The Lord, who by his resurrection has mastered the waves of suffering and persecution, rescues all those of little faith who cry out with Peter, "Lord, save me!" (14:30). Weak though his faith was, it was strong enough to cry for help.

Jesus did not have to deny Peter before the Father for denying him (Mt 10:32-33), because Peter repented. This was Peter's second conversion, his lasting conversion.

Peter was not the only one whose faith was weak. At the Last Supper, Jesus said of all his disciples, in the words of the prophet, "I will strike the shepherd and the sheep of the flock will be dispersed" (Mt 26:31, r). But after his resurrection, his own victory over tribulation, Jesus reaches out to them, grasps them by the hand, and brings them together again (Mt 28:7, 17).

"But some doubted" (Mt 28:17, r). Even the weak of faith can turn to the Lord in a second conversion and be sent forth on his mission to all nations. There is hope that the weak-faith priests and ministers of our own days can have a renewed mission. To the crucified and risen Lord we cry out with Peter, "Lord, save me!"

> The breakers of death surged round about me,
>   the destroying floods overwhelmed me. . . .
> In my distress I called upon the Lord,
>   and cried out to my God. . . .
> The earth swayed and quaked;
>   the foundations of the mountains trembled. . . .
> He reached out from on high and grasped me,
>   he drew me out of the deep waters.
>   (Ps 18:5, 7, 8, 17, n)

Fear Dispelled

Matthew's gospel, we said, is ecclesial: it was written to be read in the assembly of the Christian people. It was written in such a way that the people would respond to Jesus who is with them always, even till the end of time, living his life anew when they respond to him.

Matthew emphasizes persecution so much that we easily conclude that the storm at sea symbolized these persecutions. The disciples need not fear, for Jesus, who is with them, has calmed the sea; he has triumphed over persecution by virtue of his own death and resurrection. Throughout Matthew's gospel, Jesus is Emmanuel, God-with-us, to whom all power in heaven and on earth has been given. That is the picture of Christ that Matthew presents in the storm at sea.

The storm at sea calls to mind Psalm 46, which inspired Luther's hymn "A Mighty Fortress is our God." Apart from the name "Emmanuel" which sets the theme of Matthew's gospel (Mt 1:23), there seems to be no clear reference in Matthew to Psalm 46, whose theme is "God-with-us" in the midst of earth-shaking turmoil. The earthquakes and raging seas in the psalm symbolize social and political turmoil among the nations. During these last decades of the twentieth century, the whole world suffers from earthshaking political, economic, and social turmoil, and many people are deeply frightened. We need to read Psalm 46 (45 in the Grail Psalter) as an Emmanuel Psalm for our day.

> God is for us a refuge and strength,
> a helper close at hand, in time of distress:
> so we shall not fear though the earth should rock,
> though the mountains fall into the depths of the sea,
> even though its waters rage and foam,
> even though the mountains be shaken by its waves.
>
> The Lord of hosts is with us:
> the God of Jacob is our stronghold.

The waters of a river give joy to God's city,
the holy place where the Most High dwells.
God is within, it cannot be shaken;
God will help it at the dawning of the day.
Nations are in tumult, kingdoms are shaken:
he lifts his voice, the earth shrinks away.

> The Lord of hosts is with us:
> the God of Jacob is our stronghold.

Come, consider the works of the Lord,
the redoubtable deeds he has done on the earth.
He puts an end to wars over all the earth;
the bow he breaks, the spear he snaps.
He burns the shields with fire.
"Be still and know that I am God,
supreme among the nations, supreme on the earth!"

> The Lord of hosts is with us:
> the God of Jacob is our stronghold.
> (Ps 45, g)

The Lord Jesus, who has mastered the stormy sea in his own death and resurrection, is still with us in the turmoil of our times, saying, "Why are you afraid, O you of little faith?" (Mt 8:26).

FIVE

The Earthquake
at the Magi's Coming

Now when Jesus was born in Bethlehem of Judea in the days of Herod the king, behold, wise men from the East came to Jerusalem, saying, "Where is he who has been born king of the Jews? For we have seen his star in the East and have come to worship him." When Herod the king heard this, he was troubled, and all Jerusalem with him (Mt 2:1-3, r).

Years later, "as he [Jesus] entered Jerusalem the whole city was *stirred* to its depths" (Mt 21:10, n).

Is there a relationship between the troubling of Herod and the stirring of Jerusalem as Jesus enters it on Palm Sunday? Is Matthew's earthquake theme already at play in Herod's agitation? If so, why does Matthew use *etarachthe*, which means "troubled, agitated, terrified," when speaking of Herod, and *seio* when speaking of the agitation of Jerusalem on Palm Sunday?

Matthew uses *etarachthe* in the story of Jesus walking on the water. In this case, the word signifies sacred dread in the presence of a theophany. "But when the disciples saw him walking on the sea, they were terrified, saying, 'It is a ghost!' And they cried out in fear. But immediately he spoke to them, saying, 'Take heart. It is I. Have no fear.'" (Mt 14:26-27, r).

This is the vocabulary of theophanies, which always cause fear. In Old Testament theophanies, God usually speaks thus when he appears: "It is I! Have no fear!" The words, "It is I,"

are a play on the meaning of the holy name "Yahweh," which
means, "I who am there with you."

Terror and Judgment

The disciples are terrified as they see Jesus walking on the
water, for they are witnessing a theophany. Matthew uses the
same word to describe the agitation of Herod, and all Jerusalem with him, when the King of the Jews is mentioned. Is
Matthew hinting that Herod, too, is terrified by some sort of
theophany? Has Herod a premonition of impending judgment,
of a day of the Lord?

We saw that "earthquake," too, is a word symbolizing
theophanies. When Matthew says that "the whole city was
shaken as if by an earthquake" as Jesus comes into Jerusalem
(21:10), is he suggesting Jerusalem's impending judgment?

The judgment theme sounds in Matthew's passion narrative
as well. The events of the Lord's infancy in Matthew's second
chapter prefigure the passion. In both the infancy story and in
the passion narrative, "all the chief priests and the scribes/elders
of the people" (2:3; 27:1) take counsel against Jesus. In both
cases they assemble together with the secular ruler—with Herod
the Great in the first case (2:3) and Pilate in the second (27:2).

When Matthew tells us that Herod "assembled" the chief
priests and the scribes of the people to take counsel with him,
he uses the same word (*synagein*) which the Greek of Ps 2:2
uses to tell us how the rulers of the peoples "assemble" to
conspire against the Lord and his messiah:

> Why do the nations conspire
> and the peoples plot in vain?
> The kings of the earth set themselves,
> and the rulers take counsel together,
> against the Lord and his anointed.
> (Ps 2:2, r)

The nations and their rulers who conspire against the Lord
and his Messiah are "terrified" when the Lord sets up his king
on Mount Zion:

Then he will speak to them in his wrath,
and terrify them in his fury, saying,
"I have set up my king
on Zion my holy hill."
I will tell of the decree of the Lord:
He said to me, "You are my son,
today I have begotten you"
                    (Ps 2:5-7, r).

In Matthew's passion narrative, the rulers conspire to kill Jesus (Mt 27:1-2), and the people ratify the conspiracy: "All the people answered, 'His blood be on us and on our children!'" (Mt 27:25, r). In the Magi story, "all Jerusalem" is troubled along with Herod (2:4). So too, as Jesus enters Jerusalem, "the whole city" is shaken as if by an earthquake (21:10). Along with their rulers, "all the people," "all Jerusalem," "the whole city" are under impending judgment. They will be terrified when Jesus is established as King of the Jews in his death and resurrection. Similarly, the nations and their rulers spoken of in the psalm are terrified when the Lord's anointed proclaims his authority as king (Ps 2:7). Jesus is proclaimed "King of the Jews" when the tablet written by Pilate is affixed to the cross (Mt 27:37). This is the very same title that troubled Herod.

Matthew hints of impending judgment upon Jerusalem when he says that the whole city was shaken as if by an earthquake (21:10). He could have used the word "terrified," as he did to describe Herod's agitation. But, as we have said, like "terrified," "earthquake" is a stock word used in prophetic and apocalyptic literature to speak of theophanies, days of the Lord, days of judgment upon God's enemies. Matthew knows that Jesus, who comes as the Lord's anointed, will be rejected. Thus he lets us hear the first rumblings of the impending earthquake.

The Coming of the King

The plotters in Psalm 2 are terrified when the Lord's anointed proclaims the decree granting him divine authority to rule: "I will proclaim the decree of the Lord: The Lord said to me, 'You are my son; this day I have begotten you'" (Ps 2:7, n).

Matthew has already woven this psalm into the background of Jesus' entry into Jerusalem. First, its words are echoed in Matthew's report of the Father's words at the transfiguration of Jesus: "This is my beloved Son with whom I am well pleased" (Mt 17:5, r). After that, Jesus sets out for Jerusalem. As he enters the city, Matthew again suggests Psalm 2 to us, this time by quoting a verse from Zechariah describing the coming of the messianic king into the city: "Tell the daughter of Zion, Behold, your king is coming to you, humble, and mounted on an ass" (Mt 21:5, r; cf. Zec 9:9).

Whenever he quotes the prophets, Matthew expects that his readers will know the whole context from which the quotation was taken. In this case Zechariah is announcing the coming of the messianic king to be enthroned in the royal city Jerusalem. Just as in Psalm 2, the king will proclaim the divine decree authorizing his reign. However, whereas in Psalm 2 the king's proclamation inspires terror in the peoples of the earth, the meek and humble king in Zechariah "shall proclaim peace to the nations" (Zec 9:10, n). That is why Jesus enters the city on the peaceful ass, rather than the warlike horse.

Is Matthew's hint of judgment out of place in a scene that describes the coming of the king of peace? Not at all, for he knows that the humble king will be rejected, and the rulers will assemble to plot his death.

In Matthew 21, Jesus' entry into Jerusalem does not culminate in the proclamation of his kingship. His triumphal entry foreshadows his enthronement as king in his death and resurrection. Only then will he proclaim the divine decree establishing his kingship: "All authority in heaven and on earth has been given to me" (Mt 28:18, r). But now, his action in driving out the money changers from the temple, and his words of authority, "My house shall be called a house of prayer" (Mt 21:13, n) symbolize his full messianic authority. The "earthquake" agitation of all Jerusalem symbolizes the terror its people will experience when Jesus' kingship is fully manifested in his death and resurrection and when divine judgment is meted out by the destruction of the city at the hands of the Romans.

In Psalm 2, all the nations are struck with terror. However, in Matthew only Jerusalem and its rulers experience this terror (2:3; 21:10). For the humble Messiah proclaims peace to the nations, a message prefigured by the coming of the Magi. In God's admirable plan, the rejected Messiah becomes the cornerstone of the new and living temple. The vineyard is taken away from the rulers of Jerusalem, the wicked vinedressers, and is given to a people called together from all the nations:

> Jesus said to them, "Did you never read the scriptures, 'The stone which the builders rejected has become the keystone of the structure. It was the Lord who did this and we find it marvelous to behold?' For this reason, I tell you, the kingdom of God will be taken away from you and given to a nation that will yield a rich harvest" (Mt 21:42-43, n).

The verse about the rejected stone holds the key for interpreting everything that happened to Jesus when he came into Jerusalem as King of Peace, only to be rejected by his people. Though he is rejected, he is enthroned as King of Glory in his resurrection. The decree of royalty is proclaimed when it is nailed to the cross. "Over his head they put the charge against him, which read, 'This is Jesus the King of the Jews'" (Mt 27:37, r). This is the title that agitated Herod the Great. And certainly, as he hangs on the cross, the first tremors of the earthquake of judgment are already agitating the hearts of those who condemned him.

Terror in the Presence of God

Translators of Matthew's Greek tell us that Herod and all Jerusalem were "troubled" at the mention of the King of the Jews. They do not use the stronger meaning that this word has elsewhere, "terrified" (e.g., Dn 5:9; Mt 14:26). Are we justified, then, if we say that Matthew is comparing this "troubling" to the terror inspired by a theophany? Is Matthew presenting Herod's fear as a premonition of impending judgment?

Certainly, theophanic fear is one of Matthew's themes. The men in the boat are filled with sacred terror when Jesus walks on the water (14:26). The guards at the cross respond in holy fear at the moment of the Lord's death (27:54). The guards at his tomb are terrified when the earth quakes and the angel of the Lord rolls away the stone (28:4).

At the Lord's death, "the centurion and his men who were keeping watch over Jesus were terror-striken at seeing the earthquake and all that was happening, and said, 'Clearly this was the Son of God!'" (Mt 27:54, n). The guards express their faith in the same words used by the men in the boat, who were terrified when they saw Jesus walking on the water: "Truly, you are the Son of God" (Mt 14:33, r).

The guards at the tomb are also terrified by a theophany. "Suddenly there was a mighty earthquake, as the angel of the Lord descended from heaven. He came to the stone, rolled it back and sat on it" (Mt 28:2, n). In the Old Testament, "the angel of the Lord" always signifies a theophany. In this case, the angel sitting on the stone dramatically expresses the Lord's presence and his total victory over death.

"In appearance he resembled a flash of lightning, while his garments were as dazzling as snow. The guards grew paralyzed with fear of him and fell down like dead men" (Mt 28:3-4, n). This time the terror does not give way to a profession of faith, as it did in the case of the guards at the cross. The guards at the cross were Romans. The guards at the tomb, it seems, were Jewish temple guards. When the chief priests came to Pilate to request that he have the tomb guarded, Pilate replied, "You have a guard. Go and secure the tomb as best you can" (27:65, n). He seems to be saying, "See to it yourselves! Use your own police. Don't bother me anymore!" So the priests comply by using their own temple guard (cf. Jn 7:32, 45).

When they heard of the empty tomb, the chief priests assembled the elders of the people to conspire against the good news of the resurrection of Jesus. "When they had *assembled* with the elders and *taken counsel*, they gave a sum of money to the soldiers. . . ." (28:12, r). These guards, representing both the priests who bribed them and all the people who had concurred in the execution of Jesus, spread a lie, saying that the disciples had stolen the body of Jesus. The Roman guards at the cross, symbolizing all the nations who will come to profess their faith in Jesus, express the truth: "Truly, this was the Son of God!" (Mt 27:54, r).

Those who have rejected the theophany of the Son of God and have continued their conspiracy against the Lord and his Messiah even after his resurrection are under impending judgment. The guards' terror at the tomb forebodes the terror of the final theophany when the Lord comes as judge. The sacred fear of the guards at the cross, on the other hand, and that of the men in the boat when Jesus walks on the water, is a holy fear, which leads to faith and love. In this love and faith, they will welcome the Lord with great joy as they say at his final coming, "Blessed is he who comes in the name of the Lord!" (Mt 23:39, r).

The Handwriting on the Wall

If Herod's agitation at the mention of the King of the Jews foreboded impending judgment, why doesn't Matthew use the word for earthquake, *seio*, which he uses to express Jerusalem's foreboding when Jesus enters on Palm Sunday? Why does he use instead a word from Daniel's famous handwriting-on-the-wall scene?

In that scene, King Belshazzar of Babylon desecrates the sacred vessels from the temple in Jersualem by drinking from them at a banquet. Suddenly there is a theophany. "Opposite the lampstand, the fingers of a human hand appeared, writing on the plaster of the wall in the king's palace" (Dn 5:5, n). The handwriting pronounces judgment upon the king because of his pride and rebellion and failure to glorify the true God (Dn 5:22-23).

"Then King Belshazzar was greatly *terrified*; his face went ashen, and his lords were thrown into confusion" (Dn 5:9, n). King and counselors are frightened together. "Terrified" (*etarachthe* in the Greek of Daniel) is exactly the same word used by

Matthew for describing Herod's and his counselors' fear of the King of the Jews.

Matthew fills his account of the infancy of Jesus with allusions like this to the Old Testament. He wants the story of the handwriting on the wall to provide the background for understanding Herod's agitation at the birth of Jesus and the agitation of all Jerusalem at Jesus' entry on Palm Sunday. The apocalyptic tone characteristic of Daniel points to the coming of Jesus as the apocalyptic fulfillment. It is one of many techniques that Matthew uses to present Jesus as the fulfillment of everything in the Law, the Prophets, and the Writings. In Daniel, the handwriting on the wall is a foreboding of the coming of the Son of Man in judgment (Dn 7:10,13). For Matthew, Jesus is this Son of Man, and Herod already experiences foreboding.

Belshazzar is terrified when his wise men cannot interpret the handwriting on the wall (Dn 5:7-9). In Matthew, Herod is terrified when wise men from the East are able to read the signs given by God in the heavens and come to worship Jesus, the newborn King of the Jews. Even Herod's own wise men, the priests and scribes of the people, witness to Jesus with a verse from Micah, but they are not wise enough to act on their own witness.

The handwritings on Belshazzar's wall, interpreted by Daniel, is a message of divine judgment upon Babylon and its king:

> This is the writing that was inscribed: MENE, TEKEL, and PERES. These words mean: MENE, God has numbered your kingdom and put an end to it; TEKEL, you have been weighed on the scales and found wanting; PERES, your kingdom has been divided and given to the Medes and Persians (Dn 5:25-28, n).

Like Belshazzar, Herod is under divine judgment. At his death, not long after the coming of the Magi, his kingdom is divided into four parts. His agitation "and all Jerusalem with him" is presented by Matthew as foreshadowing the doom of Jerusalem, which comes upon her when she rejects Jesus.

Herod sees the handwriting on the wall. Indeed, he hears the clear message of Micah, the prophet: "And you, Bethlehem, land of Judah, are by no means least among the princes of Judah, since from you shall come a ruler who is to shepherd my people Israel" (Mt 2:6, n). Instead of lovingly worshipping Jesus and receiving him with joy, Herod strikes out against him in angry terror, trying to murder the God who is manifesting himself. The chief priests and elders of the people will do the same when Jesus is an adult.

But God confounds them all. Jesus escapes the murderous intent of Herod, as later he escapes death in resurrection. The Magi, symbolizing all the nations who will come to Jesus in faith, accept Jesus with loving worship. Jerusalem, which rejects him, comes under the terror of judgment: "He terrifies them in his wrath. . . . I will proclaim the decree of the Lord: the Lord said to me, 'You are my Son'" (Ps 2:5, 7, n).

But the nations hear this as a proclamation of peace:

> See, your king shall come to you;
>> a just savior is he,
>> meek and riding on an ass. . . .
> He shall proclaim peace to the nations.
> His dominion shall be from sea to sea,
>> and from the River to the ends of the earth.
>> (Zec 9:9-10, n)

"Truly, this was the Son of God!" (Mt 27:54, r).

Part II

Wholehearted Discipleship

We have seen how Jesus challenged his
disciples to follow him even into the
storm at sea. Only the Lord, the Son of
God, has the right to make such radical
demands upon human persons. Now
we shall consider the challenge which
Jesus throws out to the rich young man:
"If you would be perfect . . . come, follow me!" This will lead us to consider
the naked obedience that Jesus asks of
us all.

SIX

Wholehearted
Love of God

And behold, one came up to him, saying, "Teacher, what good deed must I do, to have eternal life?" And he said to him, "Why do you ask me about what is good? One there is who is good. If you would enter life, keep the commandments." He said to him, "Which?" And Jesus said, "You shall not kill, You shall not commit adultery, You shall not steal, You shall not bear false witness, Honor your father and mother, and, You shall love your neighbor as yourself." The young man said to him, "All these I have observed; what do I still lack?" Jesus said to him, "If you would be perfect, go, sell what you possess and give to the poor, and you will have treasure in heaven; and come follow me." When the young man heard this he went away sorrowful; for he had great possessions (Mt 19:16-22, r).

When Jesus says to the rich young man, "If you would be perfect" (Mt 19:21, r), he is not speaking merely about moral perfection. Neither is he referring simply to the basic commandments that guide our moral life. The young man says that he has already taken care of that aspect of his life. He has kept all the commandments of the law (Mt 19:20). But he still lacks something.

What Jesus therefore requires is wholeheartedness in following him: "If you want to be perfect . . . come, follow me!" The word "perfect" translates the Greek word *teleios*, which in turn corresponds to the Hebrew word *tamim*. *Tamim* means "whole, complete, sincere, wholehearted."

43

Tamim was one of the words expressing the covenant relationship between God and the people of Israel. By using this word to address the rich young man, Jesus calls him to wholehearted covenant sincerity. The Anchor Bible translates his words, "If you wish to be *true*," i.e., true to the God of Israel, true to the covenant, "follow me!" The covenant of Israel can be fulfilled only by following Jesus. Wholeheartedness in God's covenant with Israel requires a total commitment to Jesus, the Son of God, who has come as the fulfillment of the law and the prophets (Mt 5:17).

Tamim, expressing the covenant relationship, is closely akin to other covenant words, such as *hesed* ("loyal covenant love"), and *sedaqah* ("righteousness," "faithfulness to the covenant"). *Tamim* ("sincere," "wholehearted") brings out another aspect of the rich relationship between God and his people.

Jesus is calling for this same wholehearted relationship with him personally, for he is the Son of God, and he is the fulfillment of the covenant: "If you want to be wholehearted [*tamim*]. . . follow me!" (Mt 19:21).

The young man's first question to Jesus had been, "Teacher, what good deed must I do to have eternal life?" (19:16, r). Jesus does not merely require good deeds. And he does not ask just the minimum righteousness expressed by keeping the commandments. He wants *tamim*, the wholehearted, full-bodied, sincere relationship with God which is the very heart of the covenant. If you want to be wholehearted towards God, follow me!

The Hebrew Concept of Perfection

"If you would be perfect . . . come, follow me!" (Mt 19:21, r). "Perfect" is not a good translation of *teleios*, the Greek word used by Matthew, nor of *tamim*, the Hebrew corresponding to it. Words always carry many overtones. The overtones of the Greek *teleios* and the English "perfect" are quite different from the overtones of the Hebrew *tamim*.

In the Greek mentality, the perfect person was the one who by his own efforts had acquired the wholeness of virtue. He was the person who was master of himself, in complete self-possession. Perfection was a matter of gaining self-control through self-discipline. Such was the philosophy of the Greek Stoics. We must be careful not to read this meaning into the word "perfect" when it is used by Jesus.

In the biblical mentality, which is the mentality of Jesus, the person who is *tamim* (perfect) is not self-made and perfect within himself. Rather, the perfect person is one who is in sincere right relationship with God, and therefore open to the work of love which God wills to accomplish in him. Perfection is God's work in us, not something we do by ourselves. Abraham was responsible for forming his descendants in the way of righteousness so that they would be open to receiving what God had promised. "I have chosen him that he may charge his children and his household after him to keep the way of the Lord by doing righteousness and justice, so that the Lord may bring to Abraham what he has promised him" (Gn 18:19, r).

When Jesus says, "Be perfect as your heavenly Father is perfect" (Mt 5:48, r) and "If you would be perfect" (Mt 19:21, r), we miss his whole point if we give to the English word "perfect" the Greek overtones of *teleios* rather than the Hebrew overtones of *tamim*. We must therefore grasp the meaning of *tamim* in its full biblical resonance. To hear this resonance, let us study some Old Testament passages which use *tamim*.

A Right Relationship with God

"When Abram was ninety-nine years old, the Lord appeared to him and said: 'I am God the Almighty. Walk in my presence and be *blameless* [*tamim*]'" (Gn 17:1, n). The same version of the Bible had translated it, in an earlier edition, "Walk in my presence and be *perfect* (Gn 17:1,c). *Tamim*, translated either as "blameless" or "perfect," is a word meaning "complete, full, sound, without blemish, sincere, whole."

But in biblical thinking, a person is complete and whole only when he is in a right relationship with God. He is perfect and blameless only when, like Abraham, he is wholehearted in response to his Creator's call. Therefore, the best way to translate *tamim* when applied to a human person would seem to be "wholehearted." "Walk in my presence and be *wholehearted*" (Gn 17:1). Occasionally the New American Bible does translate *tamim* in that way, e.g., "Toward the wholehearted you are wholehearted" (Ps 18:26; cf. Ps 37:18, 37, n).

"Walk in my presence and be wholehearted." In the next breath, God announces the covenant that he will make with Abraham and his descendants: "Between you and me I will establish my covenant, and I will multiply you exceedingly" (Gn 17:2, n). Wholeheartedness (*tamim*) is a quality of the covenant relationship with God.

Be True to God

Tamim, as a covenant word, expresses relationship. Frequently it is used along with the preposition "toward." Thus, when Moses exhorts the Israelites to be faithful to the covenant, he says, "You, however, must be altogether sincere [*tamim*] toward the Lord, your God" (Dt 18:13, n).

Tamim, we said, does not refer merely to moral perfection within one's self. It does not refer to the Greek idea of self-acquired virtue. It expresses sincerity and truth in one's relationship with Yahweh. "You must be altogether *true* toward the Lord your God."

Moses says this in the context of his warning against sins violating the first commandment (Dt 18:9-19). Sins of fortune-telling, divining, soothsaying, use of charms, consulting ghosts and spirits—all these are sins against God's exclusive right to our worship. They violate the first commandment, "You shall have no other gods before me" (Ex 20:3, r).

One must not have a divided heart with regard to Yahweh. The God of Israel is the one God, the only God, and therefore he requires wholehearted love. "Hear, O Israel! The Lord is our God, the Lord alone! Therefore you shall love the Lord, your God, with all your heart, and with all your soul, and with all your strength" (Dt 6:4-5, n).

In the context of all of Deuteronomy, therefore, *tamim* means, "You must be altogether *wholehearted* toward the Lord, your God" (18:13). "Sincere" or "true" are good translations of *tamim* in this passage, but "wholehearted" is better, for it is a more dynamic word. It connotes some of God's own fiery, jealous love for his people, which requires a fiercely loyal love in return.

The God who requires this sincere wholeheartedness in the covenant relationship is the jealous God pictured in Exodus and Deuteronomy. He demands exclusive worship, not merely because he is the only God, but because in burning love he has rescued his people from slavery to be his own. "I am the Lord, your God, who brought you out of the land of Egypt, out of the house of bondage. You shall have no other gods before me" (Ex 20:2-3, r).

God will not share his claim for love and worship with any other power. With the passion of a lover, he demands wholeheartedness from his beloved. He is a jealous lover who cannot bear to give up Israel, his bride.

The most concise definition of the demands that Yahweh's burning zeal laid upon Israel, therefore, is expressed in Deuteronomy: "You must be altogether wholehearted toward the Lord, your God" (Dt 18:13).

When Jesus says to the rich young man, "If you want to be wholehearted . . . follow me," he means: If you want to be absolutely true and faithful to Israel's covenant relationship with her God, yield your whole person to me in wholehearted faith and love. It is not enough just to keep the commandments of the covenant. Follow me, just as Israel followed Yahweh like a bride: "I remember the devotion of your youth, how you loved me as a bride, following me in the desert, in a land unsown" (Jer 2:2, n).

In Matthew's gospel, Jesus is Emmanuel, God-with-us, calling his people back to wholehearted faithfulness to the covenant. He did not come to destroy the law and the prophets, but to fulfill them (5:17), and to restore in his people the very heart and essence of the law:

"You shall love the Lord your God with your whole heart, with your whole soul, and with all your mind." This is the greatest and the first commandment. The second is like it:

"You shall love your neighbor as yourself." On these two commandments the whole law is based, and the prophets as well (Mt 22:37-40, n).

We can be true to the God of the covenant of Israel only by following Jesus, who himself is the fulfillment of the law and the prophets.

Single-Hearted Love

The word *tamim*, wholehearted, occurs rather frequently in the psalms of "the poor of Yahweh." "The Lord watches over the lives of the wholehearted; their inheritance lasts forever. . . Watch the wholehearted man and mark the upright; for there is a future for the man of peace" (Ps 37:18, 37, n). "Blessed are they whose way is blameless [*tamim*], who walk in the law of the Lord!" (Ps 119:1, r). "May my heart be blameless [wholehearted] in thy statutes, that I may not be put to shame!" (Ps 119:80, r).

Wholeheartedness is singleheartedness in seeking the Lord alone. The sixth beatitude, "Blessed are the pure in heart, for they shall see God" (Mt 5:8, r) is well translated: "Blest are the singlehearted, for they shall see God" (5:8, n). "Where your treasure is, there your heart is also" (Mt 6:21, n). Matthew's gospel presents the religion of the heart.

Jesus invited the rich young man to this singleheartedness. "If you would be perfect, go, sell what you possess and give to the poor, and you will have treasure in heaven; and come, follow me" (Mt 19:21, r). But his invitation wasn't accepted. The man's heart was divided, "for he had many possessions." "He went away sorrowful," deprived of the happiness promised in the beatitudes. Will you also go away sad?

Listening to God

The wholeheartedness that God expects from his people is not simply a matter of avoiding a divided heart. More precisely, it is a positive listening to God alone. This is clear from

the fuller context of the words of Moses, "You must be altogether wholehearted toward the Lord, your God" (Dt 18:13).

These words act like a hinge between two tablets. One tablet
forbids listening to fortune-tellers and the like (Dt 18:9-12). The
other one commands listening to the prophet raised up by God
(18:14-19).

> Let there not be found among you . . . a fortune-teller,
> soothsayer, charmer, diviner, or caster of spells, nor anyone
> who consults ghosts and spirits or seeks oracles from the
> dead. . . . You, however, must be altogether sincere towards
> the Lord, your God. Though these nations whom you are to
> dispossess listen to their soothsayers and fortune-tellers, the
> Lord, your God, will not permit you to do so. A prophet like
> me will the Lord, your God, raise up for you from among
> your own kinsmen: to him you shall listen (Dt 18:10-15, n).

God does not speak only an occasional word to his people,
so that they are forced to go to soothsayers. No, his word of
love governs the totality of their lives. It calls for a total response, for wholeheartedness in the gift of one's person to
him.

Jesus uses that word "wholehearted" when speaking to the
rich young man. "If you want to be wholehearted, follow me!"
Jesus is the prophet that God said he would raise up. "A
prophet like me will the Lord, your God, raise up for you . . .
to him you shall listen. . . . 'I will put my words into his
mouth; he shall tell them all that I command him'" (Dt 18:15,
18, n).

Jesus is that prophet, and more than a prophet. His identity
was revealed at the transfiguration, shortly before the rich
young man came to him: "Out of the cloud came a voice which
said, 'This is my beloved Son on whom my favor rests. Listen
to him!'" (Mt 17:5, n).

Jesus is the eschatological prophet, the God-appointed inter-
preter of God's word and law. He himself is the fulfillment of
that law and the fullness of that word. More than a prophet, he
is the beloved Son. Listen to him!

And what does he say?

"Follow me!"

To be altogether wholehearted towards the Lord God, one must follow Jesus and give one's whole person to him in wholehearted commitment.

"Follow Me!"

The story of the rich young man needs to be read within the context of the Lord's journey to Jerusalem to die.

Who is this Man who requires wholehearted commitment of each person's life to him? What right does he have to ask the complete gift of self?

He is the One to whom Peter said, "You are the Christ, the Son of the Living God" (Mt 16:16, r). He is the One who said to Peter and the other disciples, "If a man wishes to come after me, he must deny his very self, take up his cross, and begin to follow in my footsteps" (16:24, n). He is the One of whom the Father said, "This is my beloved Son. . . . Listen to him!" (17:5, n).

Just after professing his faith in Jesus as Messiah (16:16), Peter refuses the message of suffering, saying to Jesus, "God forbid, Lord! This shall never happen to you" (16:22, r). In the next scene, the transfiguration, the Father responds to this refusal, saying, "This is my Beloved Son. . . . Listen to him!" (17:5, n).

Immediately after the transfiguration, Jesus again speaks about the cross (17:12) and expects believers to follow him (17:22). We must read his words to the rich young man (and to all of us) against this background. "If you want to be wholehearted, go, sell what you possess and give to the poor, and you will have treasure in heaven; and come, follow me!"

This is the only way to be *tamim*, true to the God of the covenant. Peter verifies this statement when he says in his Pentecost sermon that anyone who will not listen to Jesus will be cut off from the people of the covenant. God had said through Moses, "If any man will not listen to my words which he speaks in my name, I myself will make him answer for it"

sort of elite among God's people. "Perfect" designates disciple-ship itself. The perfect, the complete, are all those who whole-heartedly follow Christ. Jesus is simply inviting the man to become complete in the Lord, when he says, "If you would be perfect . . . follow me!" Being totally given to Jesus, following him absolutely, is the essence of Christian discipleship.

To be given to the Lord in this way necessarily entails free-dom from slavery to riches. Detachment from one's posses-sions is a necessary requirement for being a Christian. The Lord alone is the disciple's wealth. "Where your treasure is, there will your heart be also" (Mt 6:21, r).

For Jesus and for the Poor

To be a disciple of Christ, one must break free from love of riches and follow Jesus. Some disciples express this freedom by giving everything they own to the poor. Other true dis-ciples retain ownership of their possessions but express their freedom by consecrating their goods to the Lord's own love for the poor. Their service to the poor expresses the Lord's mission to the poor: "The poor have good news preached to them" (Mt 11:5, r).

When Jesus invites us to sell all, give to the poor, and follow him, the primary focus of his invitation is not on the poor, but on Jesus himself. Strip yourself of everything to follow me, he says. Make the total gift of self to me! When you give yourself to me, you must also commit yourself to my mission. Therefore consecrate your possessions to my own love and service of the poor. Whatever is given to the poor is given to me. "In so far as you did this to one of the least of these brothers of mine, you did it to me" (Mt 25:40, j).

Jesus came to fulfill the law and the prophets (Mt 5:17-18) and thereby to fulfill all righteousness (3:15). Through him, his people rediscover the heart and spirit of the law. He expresses his understanding of the heart of the law by quoting from Deuteronomy. When he is asked, "Teacher, which is the great commandment in the law?" he replies with the words, "You shall love the Lord your God with all your heart, and with all

your soul, and with all your mind." And a second is like it.
"You shall love your neighbor as yourself."

"On these two commandments," says Jesus, "depend all the
law and the prophets" (22:36-40, r). Everything else in the law
and the prophets is but the unfolding and expression of what
is contained in these two.

In these quotations from the law, Jesus goes directly to the
core of the law, namely, wholehearted response to the God of
the Covenant. Love of neighbor is inseparable from this love of
God. It is as close to the core of the Law of Moses as is wholehearted love for God.

This twofold love as lived by Jesus, and as lived by us in
Jesus, is the fulfillment of the law. Jesus challenges us to focus
this twofold love upon his own Person: "Sell all, give it to the
poor, and come, follow me!" Follow me in my self-giving on
the cross for God and for the poor.

One Question, One Answer

The story of the rich young man illustrates the truth that
Jesus came, not to abolish the law and the prophets, but to
fulfill them. Though the young man asks three questions, in
reality he is asking only one question, and Jesus gives only one
answer. He asks the second and third questions in order to
clarify Jesus' answer to the first.

The one question containing all three questions concerns
the requirements for entering into life. "Teacher, what good
deeds must I do to have eternal life?" (Mt 19:16, r). Jesus
replies, "Keep the commandments." The man asks his second
question, "Which commandments?" Jesus answers, listing the
commandments concerning love of neighbor given by Moses.
The man says, "I have kept all those," and presents his third
question, "What do I still lack?" He is still pursuing his first
question.

Jesus answers, "If you would be perfect, go, sell what you
possess and give to the poor, and you will have treasure in
heaven; and come, follow me!" (19:21, r). In the final answer,
Jesus doesn't advocate a new way, totally different from the

one indicated in his first answer, "If you would enter into life, keep the commandments" (19:17, r). Only one question was asked and one answer given. Jesus showed us the only way to eternal life.

In saying, therefore, "If you would be perfect," Jesus is not revealing a special way for a Christian elite called "the perfect." No such elite exists. His words point out the ordinary Christian way, the path down which every Christian should walk. He is inviting the young man to normal Christian discipleship. Every Christian must sell what he has and give to the poor and follow Jesus. To do this is to follow the one way to eternal life.

Eternal Life

The one question and the one answer concern Christian life: "Teacher, what good deed must I do to have eternal life?" The Greek words here translated "eternal life" mean literally "the life of the age to come"—the age of messianic fulfillment, the eschatological age, the life brought by the Messiah.

Jesus answers very simply, "If you wish to enter into *life*, keep the commandments." "Which ones?" the young man asks. Since his question refers to "the life of the age to come," in contrast to the present age, it seems that he expects new commandments for the new age. But Jesus replies by listing the commandments of the old age of the Mosaic Law. He presents a sampling from the ten commandments. In fact, he lists the second tablet of the Law—the fourth to the eighth commandments, which concern the love of neighbor (Mt 19:18-19). Then he sums it all up by adding, again from the Law of Moses, "Love your neighbor as yourself" (Mt 19:19, r; Lv 19:18, r).

Jesus agrees with Deuteronomy that the commandments are the way to life. For after all, he came not to abolish the law, but to fulfill it. Deuteronomy strongly insists that when one keeps the commandments of the covenant, one is choosing life. To refuse to keep the commandments is to choose death.

If you obey the commandments of the Lord, your God,
which I enjoin on you today, loving him, and walking in his
ways . . . you will *live* and grow numerous, and the Lord
your God will bless you in the land you are entering to
occupy. . . . I have set before you life and death, the blessing
and the curse. *Choose life*, then, that you and your descendants may live, by loving the Lord, your God, heeding his
voice, and holding fast to him (Dt 30:16, 19-20, n).

Deuteronomy speaks only of an earthly life, "a long life for
you to live on the land which the Lord swore he would give to
your fathers, Abraham, Isaac, and Jacob" (Dt 30:20, n). The
young man, however, has asked Jesus about "the life of the
age to come," the life of eschatological fulfillment brought by
the Messiah. Will the same commandments that guaranteed
life in the earthly promised land guarantee life in the kingdom
of God?

Yes, that is what Jesus said. "If you would enter life," the
life of the age to come, "keep the commandments" (Mt 19:17,
r), the same commandments that Deuteronomy lists as necessary for life in the present age.

The young man replies, "All these I have observed; what do
I still lack?" (19:20, r). Jesus' answer to this third question,
simply makes his first and second answers more precise by
pointing out the ultimate fulfillment of the commandments.
Only wholehearted love of God and neighbor as fulfilled by
Jesus himself fulfills the commandments. This wholehearted
love is the very essence of the law and the prophets. Since only
Jesus, Israel fulfilled, loves in this way, one must follow him,
one must love in the way that he loves, in order to fulfill the
law and the prophets. You are on the right way, young man,
in keeping the commandments of love. But if you want to be
perfect, if you wish to go the whole way indicated in my first
and second answers, then follow me, love in the way I love.

"Follow me" carries all the overtones of this theme as already developed in Matthew's preceeding chapters. Follow me
into the storm of life (8:22-23). Follow me in the way of the
cross (16:24). Free yourself from attachment to your posses-

sions, consecrate your belongings to my mission to the poor, consecrate to me your very power to earn a living, follow me in the way of total self-giving.

Total Self-Giving

"Hearing these words, the young man went away sad, for his possessions were many" (19:22, n). It is clear that his heart was divided; his adherence to the law was really only half-hearted. For the Law of Moses itself had required whole-heartedness in love of God: "You shall love the Lord, your God, with all your heart, and with all your soul, and with all your strength. Take to heart these words which I enjoin on you today" (Dt 6:5-6, n).

Jesus' answer to the second question, 'Which commandments?" already indicated the wholeheartedness required by the Old Law. For after quoting the commandments dealing with love of neighbor, Jesus added, "and 'love your neighbor as yourself'" (19:19, n).

These words refer deliberately to "the golden rule" in the Sermon on the Mount, where Jesus says that love of neighbor sums up all the commandments of the Law: "Whatever you wish men to do to you, do the same to them, for this is the meaning of the law and the prophets" (Mt 7:12, a). The young man says, no doubt sincerely, that he *has* loved neighbor, he *has* kept the commandments: "All these I have observed; what do I still lack?"

Does he lack love? Is his love half-hearted? If he has really kept the law and the prophets, then he loves both God and neighbor wholeheartedly (Mt 22:37-40).

Though the young man may have been wholehearted, he is challenged by Jesus to a new growth in wholeheartedness. He is invited to make a breakthrough to a new capacity and power for wholehearted love. The power to love should always be growing, and it grows only when it is expressed in a whole-hearted way. If it is rarely expressed to the fullness of its power, love will not grow to a greater fullness of power.

Or perhaps the young man has not been quite as wholehearted in love of God and neighbor as he should have been; perhaps he has not gone all the way in keeping the commandments with an overflowing love.

The man's heart is divided. It is unable to make a wholehearted response. "Hearing these words, the young man went away sad, for his possessions were many" (19:22, n). His heart was divided between the love of neighbor and the love of riches. The love of riches prevailed. A choice had to be made, for you cannot serve God and mammon. "You cannot give yourself to God and money" (Mt 6:24, n).

"You Are Not Far from the Kingdom"

In the gospel of Mark, there is a man who in many ways resembles the rich young man, but I do not think that this other man went away sad. He is the scribe who asked Jesus, "Which is the first of all the commandments?" (Mk 12:28; see also 12:29-34).

Immediately a beautiful rapport is established between Jesus and this scribe. The scribe is delighted with the answer Jesus gives to his question, and Jesus praises the scribe for his response to it. They joyfully congratulate each other for their insights and understanding. "Well spoken, Master," says the scribe. "What you have said is true: God is one, and beside him there is no other" (Mk 12:33). The scribe says this with loving reverence for that one God who has made a covenant of love with Israel. He continues, restating the words that Jesus has quoted from the Law. He clarifies them by allusions to other passages from the Law and the Prophets. In one magnificent sentence, he distills the essence of the entire Old Testament revelation: "Yes, to love him with all your heart, all your understanding, and all your strength, and to love your neighbor as yourself, is worth more than any burnt offering or sacrifice" (Mk 12:33). The reference to burnt offerings or sacrifices is an allusion to certain Old Testament passages like the one in Hosea, "For it is love that I desire, not sacrifice, and knowledge of God rather than holocausts" (Hos 6:6, n; see also Ps 40:7-9; 1 Sm 15:22).

Because the scribe sums up the law and the prophets so beautifully, Jesus commends him, saying, "You are not far from the kingdom of God" (12:34, r). The scribe's reverence for the One God of Israel seems to indicate that he not only understands that the whole law is summed up in love of God and neighbor, but that he also lives this insight. That is why Jesus can say to him approvingly, "You are not far from the kingdom of God."

The scribe might well have responded to Jesus' remark by using the words of the rich young man, "What then do I still lack?" If I am near to the kingdom, what do I need to do to enter it?

Jesus would have answered him in the same way he answered the rich young man: You are in the right way to the kingdom if you are truly keeping the commandments of love of God and neighbor. It is simply a matter now of going all the way. The New English Bible translates the words, "If you would be perfect . . . come, follow me" as, "If you wish to go the whole way . . . come, follow me!" (Mt 19:21. e).

An Expanding Heart

Throughout the story of the rich young man, we have seen that only one question is asked and one answer given. The man asks about the way into "the life of the age to come" (the age of Christ and the kingdom of God). The way, he is told, is the way of the commandments, which even in "the present age," (the age of Moses), was the way of wholehearted love of God and neighbor. The breakthrough from "not far from the kingdom" into the kingdom is simply a breakthrough from a lesser degree of love into a new wholehearted act of love, an act of total self-giving to the Lord. Only in him can we come into the life of the age to come, the Christian life "which springs up into eternal life" (Jn 4:14, c).

The wholeheartedness expressed by the Hebrew *tamim* is not static but dynamic; it is a love that should always be increasing. It should be ever expanding till at last it truly does fulfill the law and the prophets in the way that Jesus fulfilled them, in the total gift of self.

If you would be perfect, if you would not stop at the degree of love you have already reached by keeping the commandments, if you leave everything and follow me, you will break through to a marvelous new degree of wholeheartedness, a greatly increased power of wholehearted love. You will truly fulfill the law and the prophets by the total gift of self, in me and with me.

But if you refuse the challenge, you will fail in wholeheartedness. Challenges like this come repeatedly in every fervent life. The Lord needs to be chosen anew, each time with an ever greater power of love.

Jesus is speaking of a breakthrough into his own power to love to the maximum, to follow him in love to the cross. This love will increase in us infinitely, if we accept the repeated challenge to be wholehearted, if we make each new breakthrough to which we are invited.

The rich young man was on the verge of a breakthrough, but he refused the challenge. He was already in the way to life, but he failed to go all the way. He failed to enter into Jesus, whose love alone is the fulfillment of the law and the prophets, in whom alone we can come to this fulfillment.

The scribe who was "not far from the kingdom of God" probably did make the breakthrough, for everything in Mark's story about him gives the impression that he was ready and willing. He truly did love the One God of Israel, and he worshipped him with love more than with burnt offering or sacrifice (Mk 12:32-33).

But the rich young man's heart was divided. It collapsed into half-heartedness when it was offered a chance to expand. The young man returned sadly to his riches and missed the joyful blessedness of the singlehearted who see God. How many of us, like him, refuse to go all the way! We remain lukewarm in our love, because we fail to make the heroic wholehearted gift of self to Jesus when he calls us to new heights of love! We merit the reproach, "O you of little faith,!" because we refuse to let go of the created things in which we trust; we refuse to put our total trust in the Lord. Jesus is forever challenging us to let go of other things in order that we might commit our whole self to him.

EIGHT

Imitating the Father

Jesus said that the second commandment, love of neighbor, is like the first one, love of God—*like it in wholeheartedness* (Mt 22:34-40). He makes this clear in the Sermon on the Mount. Jesus teaches that we are to love our neighbors, and even enemies, with the same wholehearted love with which we love God. For when he said, "Be wholehearted as your heavenly Father is wholehearted" (5:48), he was speaking of wholehearted love of enemies as the ultimate fulfillment of the Old Testament precept, "You shall love your neighbor as yourself" (Lv 19:18):

> You have heard that it was said, "You shall love your neighbor and hate your enemy." But I say to you, love your enemies. . . . You therefore must be perfect as your heavenly Father is perfect" (Mt 5:43-44, 48, r).

"Perfect," we have seen, translates the Hebrew word *tamim*, which means complete, sincere, wholehearted. To get the full impact of the words, "Be wholehearted as your heavenly Father is wholehearted," we need to study them in the light of their full context in the Sermon on the Mount.

First, we note that these words form the punch line of an inclusion. An inclusion is a literary technique in which a passage is enclosed between two statements of the same word or idea. Mt 5:17-48, dealing with the fulfillment of the law and the prophets, is an inclusion between two uses of the word translated: "surpass," "exceed," "be more."

For I tell you, unless your righteousness *exceeds* that of the scribes and Pharisees, you will never enter the kingdom of heaven (Mt 5:20, r).

And if you salute only your brethren, what *more* are you doing than the others? (Mt 5:47, r).

The relationship between the words "exceed" (5:20) and "more" (5:47) is immediately evident in Matthew's Greek. Both derive from the same word; one is the verb and the other is the adjective form.

The word or concept that opens and closes an inclusion holds the key to interpreting the contents of the inclusion. In this case, the "including" word has been translated: "exceed," "surpass," "be more." "Unless your righteousness *exceeds* that of the scribes and Pharisees. . . . " The inclusion contains a series of six examples by which Jesus explains the surpassing righteousness expected of his followers: "You have heard that it was said. . . . But I say to you. . . ." (Mt 5:21-22; 27-28; 31-32; 33-34; 38-39; 43-48).

Jesus gives the supreme illustration of how far Christian righteousness should go. "You have heard that it was said, 'You shall love your neighbor and hate your enemy.' But I say to you, Love your enemies" (5:43). If you do not love your enemies, what *more* are you doing than others? (5:47). If you do not love your enemies, how does your righteousness *surpass* that of the Pharisees? (5:20).

The surpassing righteousness that Jesus expects of Christians, the love which is "more" than that of pagans and sinners, is measured only by the heavenly Father's own love. "You are to be wholehearted as your heavenly Father is wholehearted." The fullness of righteousness is the fullness of God's own love reproduced in his sons and daughters: "Love your enemies . . . so that you may be sons of your Father who is in heaven" (5:44-45).

This surpassing righteousness, measured only by God's own wholehearted covenant love, is the fulfillment of the law and the prophets. The entire inclusion (5:17-48) opened with the words, "Think not that I have come to abolish the law and the prophets; I have come not to abolish them, but to fulfill them" (Mt 5:17, r).

Jesus alone can fulfill the law and the prophets. The key theme of Matthew's gospel is that Jesus came "to fulfill all righteousness" (3:15, r). He is wholehearted even as the heavenly Father is wholehearted. His righteousness exceeds that of the scribes and Pharisees.

All the rest of us must follow Jesus in his fulfillment of the law and the prophets, to be wholehearted in his wholeheartedness, righteous in his righteousness. "If you would be wholehearted . . . come, follow me!" (Mt 19:21). We must follow him in the way of righteousness he accomplished by total obedience to the will of the Father. We must follow him to the cross, the way of wholehearted love.

Universal Covenant Love

We have said that the punch line to this section of Matthew is: "Be wholehearted as your heavenly Father is wholehearted." These words help us to understand the meaning of the surpassing righteousness which fulfills the law and the prophets. How is God's own wholehearted love expressed in Jesus and in his disciples? Clearly, it is expressed in the love of enemies, which is the utmost fulfillment of the love of neighbor, which sums up the law and the prophets:

> You have heard that it was said, 'You shall love your neighbor and hate your enemy.' But I say to you, Love your enemies and pray for those who persecute you, so that you may be sons of your Father who is in heaven; for he makes his sun rise on the evil and on the good, and sends rain on the just and on the unjust (Mt 5:43-45, r).

With these words, the love of neighbor commanded by the Law of Moses is expanded to include even love of enemies. "Neighbor" in the Law of Moses meant only one's fellow Israelites, one's associates in the covenant with God. "Enemy" usually meant those outside the covenant people. All these are now to be loved.

Indeed, love of neighbor is universalized to include all mankind, both the evil and the good, the just and the unjust. The Father in heaven withholds sunshine and rain from no one. He does not pick and choose those whom he will love. His love is unconditional.

It is this universal love, the Father's own wholehearted love placed within his children's hearts, that is the superabounding righteousness surpassing the righteousness of the scribes and Pharisees, and therefore fulfilling the law.

Thus God offers his covenant love to all mankind, to everyone upon whom he makes his sun to shine and his rain to fall. The covenant is expanded to invite the whole human race. This wholehearted love is indeed covenant love. For *tamim* ("wholehearted") is a covenant word. Moreover, the inclusion we have been considering deals with righteousness, a covenant quality. The exceeding righteousness, the righteousness that fulfills the law and the prophets, is God's own *tamim*, his wholehearted love poured out upon the good and evil alike.

Jesus fulfilled the law and the prophets and extended the covenant to all mankind by being wholehearted in love even as his heavenly Father was. He "fulfilled all righteousness" (Mt 3:17). In his passion story, Matthew presents Jesus as the Righteous One par excellence—the very Son of God. In the present passage, Jesus says that we too will be sons and daughters of God if our righteousness abounds in love that reaches out to the just and the unjust alike, even to enemies. Thus we will be wholehearted children of our heavenly Father.

The Blood of the Covenant

In his Eucharistic words at the Last Supper, Jesus expresses this wholehearted love and offers the covenant to all mankind, saint and sinner alike. In these words he offers his body and blood for the whole human race for the forgiveness of sins:

Then he took the cup, gave thanks, and gave it to them. "All of you must drink from it," he said, "for this is my blood, the blood of the covenant, to be poured out in behalf of many for the forgiveness of sins" (Mt 26:27-28, n).

"Many" is a Semitic idiom for "all." "The many" means "all," in contrast to "the one." Here, the many means the mass of mankind, in contradistinction to "the One" who offers his blood for them—the suffering servant who gives his life as ransom for the many (Mt 20:28, Is 53:10-12).

In the Eucharistic words that refer to the cup of his blood, Jesus indicates that he is fulfilling the prophecy of the suffering servant of Yahweh: "By his knowledgesuffering shall the righteous one, my servant, make *many* to be accounted righteous" (Is 53:12, r). By his wholehearted righteousness, Jesus makes the many righteous; he brings them back into right relationship with God. He does this by removing their guilt: "He bore the sin of many" (Is 53:12, r).

His blood is poured out for "the many" precisely "for the forgiveness of sins" (Mt 26:28). Sin is enmity towards God. The blood of Jesus is poured out to make enemies into covenant friends. Jesus practices what he preached. He loves his enemies and brings them into the covenant.

This is how Jesus is wholehearted in covenant love, even as the heavenly Father is wholehearted. The Father's sunshine and rain, poured out upon good and evil alike, are not poured out in vain. For the blood of his Son is poured out for all mankind in wholehearted love, for the forgiveness of sins. Whether or not people repent and accept this forgiveness, it remains true that the blood of Christ has been poured out for all, and the invitation to all mankind to accept the new covenant in Christ's blood still stands. The new covenant is universal in extent.

Wholehearted Toward the Wholehearted

Wholehearted love is an ever-expanding love. There is no limit to the possible growth of God's love in a human heart. God's love in the heart of his Son Jesus reached its full expression in his death on the cross. From then on, every human heart could continue to expand in the heart of Jesus towards this full degree of wholeheartedness.

This wholeheartedness of Christ contains within it all of the covenant qualities expressed in the Old Testament. It is the fullness of righteousness. It is also the fullness of covenant mercy and compassion. God's wholehearted love, which poured out the blood of his Son on the just and the unjust, is obviously a merciful love.

Perhaps this is why Luke says, "Be merciful even as your heavenly Father is merciful," rather than "Be perfect as your heavenly Father is perfect" (Lk 6:36). *Tamim,* wholehearted covenant loyalty, is so rich a concept that it takes many synonyms to express it fully. A series of such synonyms, describing God's response to the righteous, is found in Psalm 18 (the earthquake psalm of our first chapter):

> Toward the faithful you are faithful [*hesed*],
> toward the wholehearted you are wholehearted [*tamim*],
> toward the sincere you are sincere [*bawrar*]
> (Ps 18:26-27, n).

Each of these three words describing the covenant relationship is so rich in meaning that translators render them in various ways. Another version expresses the above lines in this way:

> With the loyal thou dost show thyself loyal [*hesed*];
> with the blameless man thou dost show thyself blameless
> [*tamim*];
> with the pure thou dost show thyself pure [*bawrar*]
> (Ps 18:25-26, r).

Or again:

> With the merciful thou wilt show thyself merciful [*hesed*];
> with an upright man thou wilt show thyself upright [*tamim*];
> with the pure thou wilt show thyself pure [*bawrar*]
> (Ps 18:25-26, k).

Or again:

You are loving with those who love you [*hesed*]:
You show yourself perfect with the perfect [*tamim*].
With the sincere you show yourself sincere [*bawrar*]
(Ps 17:26-27, g).

This psalm is the prayer of a righteous man, praising God for responding to his righteousness. *Hesed* ("faithful," "loyal," "merciful," "loving"), *tamim* ("wholehearted," "blameless," "upright," "perfect"), *bawrar* ("sincere," "pure"), are like so many synonyms for righteousness, which is obedience to the law of the covenant. Each expresses a different aspect of the covenant relationship.

God reveals all these covenant qualities in his covenant relationship with his faithful people. His *hesed* is faithful, loyal, merciful love. His *tamim* is the wholeness, completeness, fullness, blamelessness, wholeheartedness of this love. His love is *bawrar*, sincere, pure, singlehearted, not self-seeking, but totally concerned for his people.

Israel needed a whole set of words to express her covenant relationship with Yahweh. Perhaps "righteousness" was the basic word. Righteousness was the quality possessed by the person who always did the right thing in the covenant relationship. Whatever fostered the relationship, nourished solidarity, and fulfilled the claims of the relationship was the right thing in any given situation.

However, the requirements of God's covenant relationship with his people were spelled out in his commandments. Deuteronomy defines righteousness in terms of faithfulness to the commandments: "And it will be righteousness for us, if we are careful to do all this commandment before the Lord our God, as he has commanded us" (Dt 6:25, r).

Since the covenant relationship was a family relationship between God and his people and among the people themselves, the word *hesed* ("covenant love," "family loyalty," "kindness") added warmth and love to the basic righteousness.

But even that was not enough. One is righteous, we said,

when he fulfills all the claims that a relationship lays upon him. But what is the deepest source of Yahweh's claims upon his covenant people? It is his jealous, overflowing love. He "set his heart" upon his people and chose them in love (Dt 7:7, n), and with outstretched arm won them for himself from Egypt and from all their other foes. "You are mine!" he says (Is 43:1, n). The only fitting or righteous response to such fiery love is wholeheartedness, *tamim*. This word carries the connotation of a fiery, wholehearted, sincere love in response to God's fiery, jealous love. It is full-bodied righteousness and covenant love.

"Righteousness" and "wholeheartedness" (*tamim*) were practically synonyms. They were two ways of saying the same thing—two aspects of one reality. Often, they were used in parallelism, indicating a parity of meaning. Thus, these two qualities were ascribed to Noah. "Noah was a righteous man, blameless (*tamim*) in his generation" (Gn 6:9, r). Job is described in the same way: "There was a man in the land of Uz, whose name was Job; and that man was blameless (*tamim*) and upright, one who feared God, and turned away from evil" (Jb 1:1, r).

It is noteworthy that neither Noah nor Job was an Israelite. Noah lived before the time of Abraham and the covenant of Moses. Job was an Arabian from Uz. Yet both are praised for exemplifying the covenant qualities, righteousness and wholeheartedness (*tamim*). Both men foreshadow the fact that the Father would extend his covenant to all mankind through the blood of Jesus. As Peter later expresses it, "Truly I perceive that God shows no partiality, but in every nation any one who fears him and does what is right is acceptable to him" (Acts 10:34-35, r).

Psalm 18 seems to speak as though God has these covenant qualities only in response to the same qualities in his people: "With the wholehearted you are wholehearted, with the merciful you are merciful." Jesus puts it the other way round. His people are to be wholehearted in merciful love even as the heavenly Father is merciful in sincere, singlehearted, wholehearted love. All the covenant attributes express a mutual relationship between God and his people, a mutual, ever-deepening response to each other. Obviously, the relationship has its source in God, and in man it is always response to God. But man's response wins a deeper response from God, which in turn calls forth a deeper response from man. It is a never-ending virtuous circle. The wholehearted man has an ever-expanding heart, reaching out in ever more powerful response to the infinite wholeheartedness of God.

It all begins with God. "Be holy as I am holy," he says (Lv 19:2). The words of Jesus, "Be perfect as your heavenly Father is perfect *tamim*" (Mt 5:48, r), are modeled on these words of Leviticus, and echo also the words of Deuteronomy, "Be altogether sincere *tamim* towards the Lord, your God" (Dt 18:13, n). But Jesus' words also remind us of Psalm 18: "With the merciful you are merciful, with the wholehearted you are wholehearted, with the sincere you are sincere."

Luke, the Evangelist who emphasizes God's mercy and compassion, echoes Psalm 18 by saying, "Be merciful as your heavenly Father is merciful" (Lk 6:36). Matthew, the Evangelist who stresses wholehearted fulfillment, echoes Psalm 18 by saying, "Be wholehearted as your heavenly Father is wholehearted."

Blessed Are the Wholehearted

There is another psalm celebrating wholeheartedness. Psalm 119 could be entitled, "Blessed are the wholehearted." It begins:

> Blessed are those whose way is blameless [wholehearted,
> *tamim*],
>   who walk in the law of the Lord!
> Blessed are those who keep his testimonies,
>   who seek him with their whole heart.
>   (Ps 119:1-2, r)

The wholehearted go "all the way" in the one way that leads to life, as illustrated by the story of the rich young man. Psalm 119 sings the praises of the law, using no less than eight synonyms for law, and expresses wholehearted response to the law. Yet it is not legalistic, precisely because it is so whole-hearted. Every law coming from God points the way to the wholehearted love that fulfills the law. Thus each law points to the crucified Jesus, who is the way. This wholehearted love in Christ expands the heart till it loves with a love that is perfect even as the heavenly Father is perfect.

Sons and Daughters

Jesus fulfilled all righteousness when he sacrificed his life on the cross. By so doing, he brought righteousness to the many, either restoring them to the covenant relationship, or bringing them into this relationship for the first time. We too, by whole-heartedly loving our enemies, invite them into divine sonship, because by this love we show ourselves sons and daughters of the Father. This forgiving love is the light that shines before men and causes them to give glory to the Father in heaven. "Let your light so shine before men, that they may see your good works and give glory to your Father who is in heaven" (Mt 5:16, r).

These are the words that open the great inclusion which we have been considering. The inclusion closes with the words, "Be wholehearted even as your Father is wholehearted." This wholehearted love is the light that shines before mankind and manifests the Father's glory, for this love reflects the Father's own wholehearted love. Your good works of wholehearted love show that you are true sons and daughters of the Father (Mt 5:45), and thereby manifest the Father himself. Those who see the light of love glorify the Father by becoming his children in wholehearted love.

Wholehearted love is extended not only to enemies. It loves also the brother or sister who has offended us. It seeks out the one who has offended us, inviting him back into brotherhood and divine sonship: "If your brother sins against you, go and tell him his fault, between you and him alone. If he listens to you, *you have gained your brother*" (Mt 18:15; cf. 18:5, r).

If we cannot love our brother or sister in this way, how will we be able to love our enemies?

NINE

Naked Obedience

If you would be perfect even as your heavenly Father is perfect, follow me, Son of the Father, in my obedience to him, in my own wholeheartedness. Enter into my own exceeding righteousness. Yield your whole person to me as I have yielded my whole person to the Father, who pours out his sunshine and rain on the just and unjust, on the good and on the evil.

Only in the Son can we be sons and daughters of the Father, only in his radical obedience to the Father's will. The Father's will holds the clue to it all. Jesus says that his brothers and sisters, the sons and daughters of God, are those who do the Father's will.

"Who is my mother, and who are my brothers?" And stretching out his hand towards his disciples, he said, "Here are my mother and my brothers! For whoever does the will of my Father in heaven is my brother, and sister, and mother" (Mt 12:49-50, r).

And what is the Father's will? "Love your enemies . . . so that you may be sons of your Father who is in heaven" (Mt 5:44-45, r).

Thus we have parallel statements of the same thing:

Whoever does my Father's will is my sister and brother
and therefore child of my Father.

> Whoever loves his enemies is child of my Father
> and therefore my sister and brother.

In what manner and degree are we to love our enemies and thus do the Father's will? We must love in the same way that Jesus did. "If you want to be wholehearted as your heavenly Father is wholehearted, follow me!" To follow Jesus is to do as he did. Just as the Father pours out his rain and sunshine upon saint and sinner alike, so the Son pours out his own blood upon all mankind, to win the unjust to justice, to bring those who are evil to goodness.

Jesus taught us the Father's will not so much by word as by his own example of wholehearted obedience. "Not everyone who says to me, 'Lord, Lord,' shall enter the kingdom of heaven, but he who does the will of my Father who is in heaven" (Mt 7:21, r). "This people honors me with their lips, but their heart is far from me" (Mt 15:8, r). Only wholehearted love and obedience suffice.

You must "forgive your brother from your heart" (Mt 18:35, r). Only thus will your Father recognize you as his son or daughter and forgive you from his heart.

Jesus also expressed in words what he taught by example. His words apply his radical obedience to our lives in a practical, everyday way. The Sermon on the Mount provides a glorious sampling of our Lord's words expressing the Father's will for us. Near the end of that sermon he says, "Not everyone who says to me, 'Lord, Lord,' shall enter the kingdom of heaven, but he who does *the will of my Father* who is in heaven." He adds, "Everyone then who hears *these words of mine* and does them will be like a wise man who built his house upon the rock" (Mt 7:24, r). *These words of mine* express *the will of my Father*.

Behind all these words we must see Jesus' obedience to his Father. His words form a portrait of him. They show us his radical gift of himself to the Father's will in wholehearted love.

Everything Jesus said is verified in his own person. "Follow me" means "Do as I say," but even more it means "Do as I do, live as I live, obey as I obey." A true disciple lives with his teacher, shares his life, and learns by living with him.

That is why after showing the disciples relating to Jesus as Teacher, Matthew shows them yielding to him as Lord, sharing his life, following in the way that he went. Righteousness exceeding that of the scribes and Pharisees consists, not just in accepting the words of the Teacher, but in lovingly surrendering self to him and living the way that he did.

In everything he asks us to do, we must see a living portrait of Jesus himself. When he insists that John baptize him so that they might fulfill all righteousness, Jesus is saying that he must be baptized in obedience to the Father's will. His baptism in the Jordan symbolizes his coming baptism of suffering on the cross. In scripture, immersion in overwhelming floods of water always symbolizes great suffering.

We must fulfill righteousness together, Jesus tells John. "Let it be so now; for thus it is fitting *for us* to fulfill all righteousness" (Mt 3:15, r). In Matthew's ecclesial gospel, these words are to be heard by the people from every nation who are baptized in the Name of the Father and of the Son and of the Holy Spirit (Mt 28:19). The words are addressed to all of them, for they are baptized into Christ's own righteousness, and in him and with him they fulfill all righteousness. They follow him through the storm at sea, through his earthquake into his new creation, through his death into his resurrection.

"John came to you in the way of righteousness" (Mt 21:32, r). John's death pointed the way to the cross and death of Jesus. By his martyrdom, he witnessed to the coming martyrdom of Jesus. With Jesus he fulfilled all righteousness. He pointed out that we must all be martyrs with Christ. We must be baptized into his baptism. With Jesus, like John, we must make the gift of our lives in radical obedience to the Father's will.

In the Face of Temptation

The scene of Christ's temptations in the desert shows Jesus living only according to the Father's will: "Man shall not live by bread alone, but by every word that proceeds from the mouth of God" (Mt 4:4, r). His divine sonship is put to the test in these temptations: "If you are the Son of God, command these stones to turn into bread" (4:3, n). By resisting the temptations, and doing the Father's will, he is shown indeed to be God's Son.

This temptation scene foreshadows the testing of his sonship as he hangs on the cross: "If you are the Son of God, come down from the cross" (Mt 27:40, r). Again he resists the temptation, and by remaining in the Father's will, he is manifested as Son of the eternal Father: "Truly, this was the Son of God!" (27:54, r).

Obedience was no easier for Jesus than for any other son or daughter of God. We see him struggling with his Father's will: "My Father, if it be possible, let this cup pass from me; nevertheless, not as I will, but as thou wilt" (Mt 26:39, r). By submitting, he gives himself to the Father in radical obedience, an obedience that does not merely fulfill this command or that one, but that yields his whole life and being to God. It is naked obedience to the Father's naked will.

Jesus asks this same naked obedience of all his disciples. Exceeding wholehearted righteousness does not consist in keeping this commandment or that one, or even all the commandments of the law. The rich young man had kept them all, but Jesus asked more than that: "Follow me!" Make the radical gift of your whole person to me, and in my obedience give yourself to the Father.

Jesus' whole life is a living word that calls for radical obedience like his own. The practical ways of expressing this total gift of self in everyday living are made clear in the words of Jesus.

For example, we noted that the Sermon on the Mount contains an inclusion, the theme of which is wholehearted righteousness exceeding that of the scribes and Pharisees. This Christian righteousness is a love that extends even to enemies. The inclusion contains six examples of this love. Each example is introduced with the formula, "You have heard it said . . . but I say to you" (Mt 5:21-44). In each of these examples, we need to see Jesus himself. We must see these examples as down-to-earth ways of living according to the Son's naked obedience to the Father, his wholehearted radical gift of self to God.

If They Take Your Shirt

In one of these examples, Jesus tells us: If they take your shirt, let them have your coat also; if they strike you on one cheek, turn the other to them also. Jesus himself did this. They stripped him of everything, and he died naked. Will you follow him in this? Will you exclude all vindictiveness from your life? Will you persevere in the faith and in loving your enemies even when they persecute you?

Let us compare the words of Jesus with the portrait of Jesus behind the words.

The words:

> You have heard that it was said, "An eye for an eye and a tooth for a tooth." But I say to you, Do not resist one who is evil. But if anyone strikes you on the right cheek, turn to him the other also; and if anyone would sue you and take away your coat, let him have your cloak as well; and if anyone would force you to go one mile, go with him two miles (Mt 5:38-42, r).

The portrait of Jesus behind the words:

> And they spat upon him, and took the reed and struck him on the head. And when they mocked him, they stripped him of the robe, and put his own clothes on him, and led him away to crucify him. . . . And when they had crucified him, they divided his garments among them by casting lots (Mt 27:30-31, 35, r).

Jesus was stripped not only of his clothing, his human dignity, and of the respect due him as a man who deserved to be listened to. He was stripped even of his friends and of every human support. In his moment of greatest need, in the Garden of Olives, his friends fell asleep. Then they abandoned him and denied they knew him.

Not only was he stripped of his friends and followers, he was not even to be comforted by his Father's presence. In desolation he cries out, "My God, my God, why hast thou forsaken me?" (Mt 27:46, r).

Yet throughout it all he remains the Son of God, totally focused upon the Father, and accepting the Father's will until the very end. His cry of dereliction, "My God, my God, why hast thou forsaken me?" is a cry of filial hope and trust. Had he given up all hope, he never would have uttered this prayer.

He died naked, in naked obedience, stripped of everything, yielding himself to the Father, trusting in the Father's will, in openness to the Father's purposes.

Like Abraham

This was the kind of righteousness that God told Abraham to teach his children, a righteousness perfectly open and obedient to what God wills to accomplish in his people:

> Shall I hide from Abraham what I am about to do?. . . No, for I have chosen him, that he may charge his children and his household after him to keep the way of the Lord by doing righteousness and justice; so that the Lord may bring to Abraham what he has promised him (Gn 18:17, 19, r).

The righteousness that consists of obedience to the covenant law opens the way for God to accomplish in his people what he had promised to do for Abraham. Obedience is simply openness to God's glorious work in us.

Already from Abraham God required naked obedience. Abraham had to be stripped of everything—not only his homeland, which he had to leave in answer to God's call, but even his beloved son, Isaac, who was his total hope. He was asked to offer this beloved son in sacrifice, trusting only in God's will. He had to respond to God's naked will—not as expressed in specific promises made to him or in specific commands that he could understand and fulfill or in something easy to grasp and carry out—but God's inexpressible will, which surpasses all understanding.

To this naked will, not clothed in terms we can grasp, we must yield ourselves in naked obedience, stripped of desire for what we might think is God's purpose for us. His purposes surpass all our imaginings. We must be emptied of the lesser to be filled with the greater.

Trust

God's people experience the call to naked obedience in various ways. The most radical way of all, of course, is when one finds oneself face-to-face with death. A man finds himself being eaten up with cancer, for example, and prays to God for healing. He hopes that God's will for him will be a complete cure. Yet sometimes the heavenly Father does not grant such a healing when it is requested. Or perhaps he delays the healing, and the man continues to pray for it. The longer the healing is delayed, the more the man is forced to yield to the unknown will of God. Does the Father will this cure or doesn't he? The man does not know.

He needs to make the naked obedience of Jesus his own. As he continues to pray, he can only say with Jesus: "My Father, if it be possible, let this cup pass from me; nevertheless, not as I will, but as thou wilt. . . . My Father, if this cannot pass unless I drink it, thy will be done" (Mt 26:39, 42, r).

The man strips himself of his own will and yields to the Father's will, whatever that might be. Quite possibly, the Father's will is something other than what the man would like. Perhaps it is the Father's will that he die and return to the dust from which he was created.

Sooner or later every one of us must face unflinchingly the disturbing truth that before God we are but dust and ashes. He who created us from dust orders us to return to dust. "You turn man back to dust, saying, 'Return, O children of men'" (Ps 90:3, n).

Yet we must face the whole truth, not just that we must

return to dust, but that God is our Father and we his sons and daughters. Even as we realize that it may not be our Father's will to cure us, we must accept the reality that he is our Father, and we trust him as such: "As a father has compassion on his children, so the Lord has compassion toward those who fear him. For he knows how we are formed, he remembers that we are dust" (Ps 103:13-14, n).

Psalm 90 expresses this even more powerfully. The author of the psalm trusts unflinchingly in God's love and mercy even while he confesses that God commands man to return to the dust from which he was created:

O Lord, you have been our refuge through all
    generations . . .
You turn man back to dust, saying,
"Return, O children of men" (Ps 90:1, 3, n).

The psalmist fully realizes that this return to dust is the penalty of man's sinfulness:

Truly we are consumed by your anger,
    and by your wrath we are put to rout.
You have kept our iniquities before you,
    our hidden sins in the light of your scrutiny (Ps 90:7-8).

Yet with full faith and trust, he turns God's words back upon him. To God who said, "Return to dust, you children of men," the psalmist says, "Return to us!"

Return, O Lord! How long?
Have pity on your servants!
Fill us at daybreak with your kindness,
    that we may shout for joy and gladness all our days
                                                    (Ps 90:13-14, n).

By trusting in God, man does not deny his condition as a sinner doomed to die, but neither does he forget the Father's merciful love. It is necessary that rebel man experience fully his nothingness in the presence of the divine majesty. For in sinning, man tries to usurp the place of God: "Your eyes will be opened, and you will be like God!" (Gn 3:5, r). The remedy for our pride is the full experience of our nothingness as dust and ashes: "You are dust, and to dust you shall return" (Gn 3:19, r).

Only in the full truth of our condition as dust and ashes does our act of faith in God our Father have its full force. He who created us from dust and orders us to return to dust will call us forth again from dust to resurrection.

Simultaneously, then, we must witness to two aspects of one truth: We are but dust and ashes before the Lord our God, and yet we are sons and daughters of this God, our Father.

Peter stepped out of the boat to walk on water, but he began to sink when he saw the power of the winds. He cried out, "Lord, save me!" (Mt 14:30). Peter's experience is verified most fully in our lives in the experience of death. As death approaches, we must step out in faith, saying, "Lord, save me!" "Jesus at once stretched out his hand and caught him" (Mt 14:31, n).

Wholehearted Love in Marriage

Jesus says: Follow me in naked obedience. After our initial response to this call, we must continue to express our obedience in daily practical ways. Let us return to the examples we find in the Sermon on the Mount.

Wholehearted Christian righteousness, exceeding that of the scribes and Pharisees, goes so far that it loves even enemies. Surely then it loves also those closest to us, such as a husband or wife. Jesus illustrates abounding Christian righteousness with an example from married life:

It was also said, "Whoever divorces his wife, let him give her a certificate of divorce." But I say to you that everyone who divorces his wife, except on the grounds of unchastity an incestuous union makes her an adulteress; and whoever marries a divorced woman commits adultery" (Mt 5:31-32, r).

Some Christians interpret this "unchastity" (*porneia* in Matthew's Greek) as "adultery," and they permit divorce in this case. But Matthew could not possibly mean that. When speaking of adultery, he uses another word, *moicheia* (15:19). Whatever Matthew means by *porneia*, he does not mean adultery. Most likely he gives the word the meaning that it has in Acts (15:20, 29), where it refers to incestuous unions, unions within certain degrees of kinship or legal relationship forbidden in Lv 18:6-18. For Paul, *porneia* means incest: "It is actually reported that there exists among you *porneia*, and such *porneia* as does not exist among pagans, that a man should have his father's wife" (1 Cor 5:1).

Matthew seems to be saying that converts to Christianity should break off those illegal incestuous unions, which in his eyes were not marriages. In doing this, they would not violate Jesus' prohibition of divorce.

Divorce came into existence, says Jesus, not from God, but from human hardness of heart, which is the very antithesis of the wholehearted love that characterizes Christian righteousness. "For your hardness of heart Moses allowed you to divorce your wives, but from the beginning it was not so" (Mt 19:8, r).

"Hardness of heart" (*sklero-kardia*) means an obstinate refusal to respond to God's promptings. It is disobedience to his inspirations. It shows that one has refused to commit his life to the Lord in radical obedience. This hardness is a rather persistent theme in the scriptures. Jesus became angry with those who stubbornly resisted him and found fault with his healings on the sabbath: "He looked around at them with anger, grieved at their hardness of heart" (Mk 3:5, r). "O that today you would hearken to his voice! Harden not your hearts as at Meribah" (Ps 95:7-8, r).

Hardness of heart is the cause of divorce. It is a resistance not only to the spouse but to God. It is disobedience to the will of the Creator, who did not create divorce.

Have you not read that he who made them from the beginning made them male and female, and said, "For this reason a man shall leave his father and mother and be joined to his wife, and the two shall become one?" So they are no longer two, but one. What therefore God has joined together, let no man put asunder (Mt 19:4-6, r).

Is not a heart hardened against one's spouse hardened also against God, who created marriage to be a permanent union in wholehearted love? If Christians, perfect as their heavenly Father is perfect, love even their enemies, then certainly they can "forgive from the heart" a spouse who has offended them (Mt 18:35, r). Hardness of heart cannot develop where there is Christian forgiveness.

Married couples follow Christ wholeheartedly by practicing wholehearted receptive love for each other. "If you would be wholehearted, strip off your resentments against your spouse, and come, follow me!" Love from the heart!

"Be Reconciled with Your Brother"

Murder and unrighteous anger are excluded from Christian life precisely because we are brothers and sisters, loving each other wholeheartedly with the Father's wholehearted love.

You have heard that it was said to the men of old, "You shall not kill; and whoever kills shall be liable to judgment." But I say to you that every one who is angry with his brother shall be liable to judgment (Mt 5:21, r).

The word "brother" occurs repeatedly throughout this passage. We cannot come into our Father's presence without being reconciled to our brother.

If you are offering your gift at the altar, and there remember that your brother has something against you, leave your gift there before the altar and go; first be reconciled to your brother, and then come and offer your gift (Mt 5:23-24, r).

Our commitment to the Father in naked obedience must be expressed in our commitment to brothers and sisters in whole-hearted love.

"Adultery in His Heart"

If the Father pours out his rain and sunshine upon all mankind because all are his children, surely this same love must pour forth from our hearts. The abounding Christian righteousness which is wholehearted love, like the heavenly Father's wholehearted love for his children, treats every one of God's children with the greatest reverence and respect.

You have heard that it was said, "You shall not commit adultery." But I say to you that everyone who looks at a woman lustfully has already committed adultery with her in his heart (Mt 5:27, r).

Christian chastity is fundamentally a profound reverence for the dignity of every person and for the source of human life. Every person is created to be a child of God and is meant to live with God forever. By the mere fact that a person exists in human nature, divine life is offered to him through the blood of Christ. Whether the offer is accepted or rejected, God continues to love this person, and his offer of divine life to him remains until it is irrevocably rejected by the sin of final impenitence.

For these reasons, every human person, whether saint or sinner, is to be loved with God's own love, and all human life, even the most undeveloped life in the womb, is to be treated with God's own fatherly reverence. This reverence is to be extended even to the powers of generation which produce new life. This reverence for the dignity of human life and for its source is a fundamental element in Christian chastity.

The abounding righteousness of God's children takes advantage of no one. Lust in thought or desire or action is a desecration of a child of God and a violation of the wellsprings of life.

"Do Not Swear"

Again you have heard it said to the men of old, "You shall not swear falsely, but shall perform to the Lord what you have sworn." But I say to you, Do not swear at all. . . . Let what you say be simply "Yes" or "No"; anything more than this comes from evil (Mt 5:33, 37, r).

Where love is completely sincere, mutual trust and confidence flourish. Wholehearted love eliminates the need for oaths. There is no insincerity which needs to mask itself behind false oaths. With the sincere, it is easy to be sincere. Where there is trust, it is easy to trust.

Toward Jerusalem

Matthew's ecclesial gospel depicts the disciples following Jesus in his naked obedience. In the church assembly, Matthew retells the life of Jesus in such a way that all Christian believers become fully involved in the Lord's journey of obedience. When Jesus tells them that he must go up to Jerusalem to die (16:21), Peter objects to this kind of Messiah (16:22). But Jesus insists, "If any man would come after me, let him deny himself and take up his cross and follow me" (16:24, r).

The disciples assemble to begin the journey with Jesus. "While they were *gathering* in Galilee, Jesus said to them, 'The Son of Man is about to be betrayed into the hands of men, and they will kill him, and on the third day he will be raised.' And they felt deeply distressed" (Mt 17:22-23, m). In this passage, Matthew, as usual, is thinking of the church assembly. All Christians have been *gathered* together to follow Jesus in his journey of obedience. And we feel deeply distressed, not so much because Jesus is to be betrayed and killed, but because we have been called to follow him in this way. The radical obedience he asks is hard to take!

Jesus makes his journey up to Jerusalem. This is the Son's supreme act of obedience to his Father. He comes in naked obedience to the Father's will. For he knows full well that he comes to die. Even before he started on this last journey, he knew that he faced certain death in Jerusalem. "From then on" from the time of Peter's confession that Jesus is the Messiah Jesus *the Messiah* started to indicate to his disciples that he must go to Jerusalem and suffer greatly there, . . . and to be put to death" (Mt 16:21, n).

Why does this particular translation, following several ancient manuscripts, have the words "the Messiah?"

Peter has just confessed that Jesus is the Messiah, God's Anointed. Jesus commends Peter for this God-given insight (Mt 16:17). He is fully conscious that he is the Messiah. Precisely in his capacity as Messiah he goes up to Jerusalem in obedience to his messianic commission, his divine anointing. "From then on, Jesus *as Messiah*" goes up to the city (16:21).

As they drew near Jerusalem, Jesus sent two of his disciples to bring the animal he would ride into the city.

They brought the ass and the colt and laid their cloaks on them, and he mounted. The huge crowd spread their cloaks on the road, while some began to cut branches from the trees and lay them along his path. The groups preceding him as well as those following kept crying out: "Hosanna to the Son of David. Blessed is he who comes in the name of the Lord! Hosanna in the highest!" (Mt 21:8-9, n).

Though his whole journey up to Jerusalem is his supreme act of obedience to the One who anointed him, this act has to be renewed again and again as he lives out his initial commitment to the Father's will. We too have to renew repeatedly our gift of self to the Lord as new situations call for renewed obedience. Later we see Jesus struggle during the agony in the garden as he renews his acceptance in the most radical way possible. Through this acceptance, he fulfills all righteousness. The fullness of righteousness is the total surrender of one's whole being to God in naked obedience.

Part III

The Rejected Stone

Fully conscious that he is the Messiah, commissioned by the Father, Jesus makes his obedient journey to Jerusalem. The Messianic King enters his capital. His coming issues a final challenge to his people to accept him as God's Anointed One. However, to accept an obedient Messiah means to practice radical obedience like his own. His people are unwilling. They reject him and put him to death.

TEN

The Liturgy at the Gate

Matthew, chapter 21, consists of an inclusion between two references to Psalm 118. At the beginning of the chapter, the people welcome Jesus into Jerusalem, acclaiming him with the words of the psalm, "Blessed is he who comes in the name of the Lord" (Ps 118:26, r; Mt 21:9). The chapter ends with words of the same psalm that speak of Jesus' rejection by the people, "The stone which the builders rejected has become the keystone of the structure" (Ps 118:22; Mt 21:42).

As we have said, the opening and closing verses of an inclusion hold the key to the interpretation of everything included between them. Psalm 118 is a liturgy at the gate, and the whole of chapter 21 can be interpreted as a fulfillment of the Old Testament liturgies at the gate. In a special way, Jesus' entry into Jerusalem fulfills the royal enthronement liturgies, which include a solemn procession of the kings of Judah through the city gates to take possession of their royal city.

Jesus, the Messianic King, "Son of David" (Mt 21:9), enters his royal city. He is acclaimed by the people, "Blessed is he who comes in the name of the Lord." But he is rejected by the ruling class, the chief priests, and the scribes (21:15). He is "the stone which the builders rejected" (21:42). Later on, the people will ratify this rejection: "The whole people said in reply, 'Let his blood be on us and on our children'" (Mt 27:25, n).

"Let his blood be on us." As usual in his ecclesial gospel, Matthew expects his readers to identify with these words.

"The whole people" becomes a symbol of all mankind, which indeed has shed the blood of Jesus by its sins. All of us, in our confession of our sinfulness, admit that we are responsible for the death of Jesus.

But all of us must also repeat the words in a new way: "Let his blood be on us and on our children for the remission of our sins." At the Last Supper, Jesus said, "This is my blood, the blood of the covenant, to be poured out in behalf of many for the forgiveness of sins" (Mt 26:28, n).

What deep meaning of the Lord's death and resurrection does Matthew teach by referring to the liturgy at the gate in Psalm 118?

Through Gates of Justice

The liturgy at the gate consisted of a question and answer ritual that took place at the entrance to the temple at Jerusalem. Coming to the gates in solemn procession, the people sought admission to God's house on the holy mountain. They asked what was required of them for admission into the divine presence. "Who can ascend the mountain of the Lord? Or who may stand in his holy place?" (Ps 24:3, n). From inside, the keepers of the gates answered, "He whose hands are sinless, whose heart is clean, who desires not what is vain, nor swears deceitfully to his neighbor" (Ps 24:4, n).

These liturgies at the gate invite from the hearts of the people a declaration of loyalty to God's will for justice among his covenant people. If they are to remain in communion with God, the people must practice the justice pledged in this liturgy:

Lord, who shall be admitted to your tent
and dwell on your holy mountain?
He who walks without fault;
he who acts with justice
and speaks the truth from his heart;
he who does not slander with his tongue;
he who does no wrong to his brother,

who casts no slur on his neighbor,
who holds the godless in disdain,
but honours those who fear the Lord;
he who keeps his pledge, come what may;
who takes no interest on a loan
and accepts no bribe against the innocent.
Such a man will stand firm forever
(Ps 14, g).

The second verse, "he who walks without fault, he who acts with justice," again brings out the inseparability of wholeheartedness and righteousness. "Without fault" translates the Hebrew *tamim* (wholeheartedly). "He who walks wholeheartedly" is practically synonymous with "he who acts with justice." The verses that follow identify this wholeheartedness towards God with justice towards neighbor. One cannot be right with God and wrong with his fellowmen. One can enjoy friendship with God only if he is just towards neighbor.

Therefore the temple gates are called "the gates of justice" (righteousness) (Ps 118:19, n), for only the righteous may pass through them. "This gate is the Lord's; the just shall enter it" (Ps 118:20, n). Peace and security are the fruits of wholehearted righteousness. "Such a man will stand firm forever" (Ps 15:5, g).

"A strong city have we; he sets up walls and ramparts to protect us" (Is 26:1, n). The city's security is founded on the stability of the righteous relationships of its citizens. These relationships are built upon firm trust in God and faithfulness to him.

Open up the gates to let in a nation that is just,
    one that keeps faith.
A nation of firm purpose you keep in peace,
    in peace, for its trust in you.
Trust in the Lord forever!
    for the Lord is an eternal Rock.
(Is 26:2-4, n)

Righteousness is first of all rightness with God in faith, fidelity, and trust. Trusting in the Lord, the eternal Rock, brings peace and security. Building upon this Rock, God's people build justice into their human relationships, and thus their city is strong and safe: "Justice will bring about peace, right will produce calm and security" (Is 32:17, n).

Jesus fulfills the righteousness spoken of in the gate liturgies. He is the one who came "to fulfill all righteousness" (Mt 3:15, r). Those who entrust themselves to him also fulfill righteousness. We have seen that the exceeding righteousness required for entering the kingdom (5:20), consists in accepting Jesus and surrendering self to his radical claim upon our life, and following him in wholehearted love and justice.

The just, when they come to the gates of God's house, are received favorably by God, who grants them his friendship: "Such is the race that seeks for him, that seeks the face of the God of Jacob" (Ps 24:6, n). "The face of God" signifies his good will, presence, friendship. The just, who seek his face, find it. They are admitted to his presence and live in his friendship. The Lord pours out on them the blessings of the covenant: "He shall receive a blessing from the Lord, a reward from God his savior" (Ps 24:5, n).

Psalm 118—A Gate Liturgy

In Psalm 118, too, the pilgrims to the Feast of Tabernacles are called "the just." There is rejoicing "in the tents of the just" (Ps 118:15, n). These are the tents made of leafy bows in which the pilgrims dwell throughout the festival. During the celebration they carry leafy bows in liturgical procession to "the gates of justice" (Ps 118:19). "Join in procession with leafy boughs up to the horns of the altar" (Ps 118:27, n).

In a special way the king, the representative of all the people, receives a blessing at the "gates of justice" (Ps 118:19, n). He says, "Open to me the gates of justice; I will enter them and give thanks to the Lord" (Ps 118:19, n). Though the king utters these words, he is acting on behalf of the whole people. He is responsible for establishing and maintaining justice among all his people. "In his enduring love for Israel, the Lord has made you king to carry out judgment and justice" (1 Kgs 10:9, n). "O God, with your judgment endow the king, and with your justice, the king's son; he shall govern your people with justice and your afflicted ones with judgment" (Ps 72:1-2, n).

When the king, in the name of all the people, seeks admission through the gates of justice, the keepers of the gate respond, "This gate is the Lord's; the just shall enter it" (Ps 118:20, n).

Jesus Enters through the Gates

Against this Old Testament background of the liturgy at the gate, we must read Matthew's account of Jesus' entrance into Jerusalem and the temple (Mt 21:1-13). Matthew quotes a verse from Psalm 118 to tie the scene in with the traditional gate liturgies. As Jesus approaches the gates of the city, the people greet him with the words of the psalm which the priests addressed to the king when he asked that the gates of justice be opened to him: "Blessed is he who comes in the name of the Lord!" (Ps 118:26; Mt 21:9).

Jesus is fully qualified to pass through the gates of justice into the presence of God. Matthew's theme throughout his gospel is that Jesus fulfills all justice: "For thus it is fitting for us to fulfill all righteousness" (Mt 3:15, r). Jesus fulfills all righteousness by perfectly obeying the Father's will, not only by coming to the Jordan to be baptized in a symbolic ceremony prefiguring his sacrificial death, but by coming to Jerusalem where he will be rejected and put to death by his own people. By that very death he will save his people from their sins and restore them to righteousness.

It is the king's responsibility to bring about justice among his people. By showing how Jesus is welcomed into the city through the gates of justice, Matthew wants us to see Jesus as the one who fulfills the office of the king—the one who comes "to fulfill all righteousness" (Mt 3:15, r). Not only does he fulfill justice by his perfect obedience to the Father, but he communicates this justice to all the nations as the fruit of his own obedience. "He will proclaim justice to the nations," says Matthew, showing that the mission of the Servant of Yahweh is fulfilled by Jesus (Mt 12:18, n; Is 42:1).

As he comes to the gates, Jesus is rightly acclaimed as Messiah: "Hosanna to the Son of David! Blessed is he who comes in the name of the Lord! Hosanna in the highest!" (Mt 21:9, n). He is that Son of David foretold by Jeremiah. His symbolic "throne name" is "the Lord our Justice" (Jer 23:5-6, n), and he in turn gives this name to the holy city, the people of God (Jer 33:14-16, n). He communicates to them his own justice:

> Behold, the days are coming,
> says the Lord,
> when I will raise up
>   a righteous shoot to David;
> As king he shall reign
>   and govern wisely,
> he shall do what is
>   just and right in the land.
> In his days Judah shall be saved
>   Israel shall dwell in security.
> This is the name they give *him*
>   "The Lord our Justice"
>   (Jer 23:5-6, n).

> The days are coming, says the Lord, when
> I will fulfill the promise I made to the
> house of Israel and Judah.
> In those days, in that time,
> I will raise up for David
>   a just shoot;
> He shall do what is
>   right and just in the land.
> In those days Judah shall be safe
>   and Jerusalem shall dwell secure;
> This is what they shall call *her*:
>   "The Lord our Justice"
>   (Jer 33:14-16, n).

ELEVEN

Tell the Daughter of Zion

Who else, besides the just, enters through the gates of justice?
Yahweh, the King of Glory!

> O gates, lift high your heads;
> grow higher, ancient doors.
> Let him enter, the king of glory!

> Who is the king of glory?

> The Lord, the mighty, the valiant,
> the Lord, the valiant in war.

> O gates, lift high your heads;
> grow higher, ancient doors.
> Let him enter, the king of glory!

> Who is he, the king of glory?

> He, the Lord of armies,
> he is the king of glory
>   (Ps 23:7-10, g).

The psalmist depicts the gateway as being too low for the great God to enter. He commands that the lintels raise up. In a similar manner, the psalmist invites us to open our hearts wide to receive the Lord. No doubt Psalm 24 (23 in the Grail Psalter) celebrated a liturgy commemorating the original placement of the Ark of the Covenant in the temple. The Ark signified God's own presence. The Lord comes to his temple to dwell, so that his just ones might meet him in friendly communion. The King of Glory, Yahweh himself, comes into his temple.

In Matthew's account of Jesus' entrance into the city and the temple, two Old Testament passages are recast into one. One of the passages refers to the coming of Yahweh (Is 62:11). The other refers to the coming of the Messianic King, the Son of David (Zec 9:9). By combining the two (Mt 21:5), Matthew indicates that the coming of Jesus, the Son of David is the coming of Yahweh, the King of Glory.

> Say to daughter Zion
> Your savior comes (Is 62:11, n).

> Rejoice heartily, O daughter Zion,
> Shout for joy, O daughter Jerusalem!
> See, your king shall come to you,
> A just savior is he,
> Meek, and riding on an ass (Zec 9:9, n).

> Tell the daughter of Zion
> Your king comes to you
> Humble, riding an ass (Mt 21:5).

In Isaiah, the savior who comes is Yahweh, the Lord. The passage from which this verse is taken (62:6-12) is like a liturgy at the gate. Though Jerusalem lies in ruins, and rubble chokes her gates (62:10), those hoping for her restoration are pictured as watchmen on her walls, waiting and expecting the Lord's coming, ardently praying, giving him no peace till he comes to restore the city:

> Upon your walls, O Jerusalem,
>   I have stationed watchmen;
> Never, by day or by night,
>   shall they be silent.
> O you who are to remind the Lord,
>   take no rest And give no rest to him,

until he re-establishes Jerusalem
And makes it the pride of the earth.
(Is 62:6-7, n)

In answer to these prayers, the order goes out to clear away the rubble so that Yahweh may come through, leading his people:

Pass through, pass through the gates,
   prepare the way for the people;
Build up, build up the highway, clear it of stones,
   raise up a standard over the nations.
See, the Lord proclaims to the ends of the earth:
   Say to daughter Zion, your savior comes!
(Is 62:10-11, n)

Matthew says that this passage is fulfilled when Jesus comes through the gates as Messianic King to restore his people (Mt 21:5). He makes this point by quoting but one phrase from Isaiah's passage, "Tell the daughter of Zion" (Is 62:11), and merging it with the words of Zechariah, which refer to the coming of the Son of David, the Messianic King. Zion's restoration, sall the nations: "Raise up a standard over the nations. . . . Say to daughter Zion, your savior comes!" (Is 62:10-11, n). Jesus is this hope of the nations: "In his name, the Gentiles will find hope" (Mt 12:21, n; Is 11:10 fused with 42:4).

The Royal Enthronement

Matthew says that Jesus' entrance into Jerusalem also fulfills a passage from Zechariah, from which he quotes one verse (Zec 9:9; Mt 21:5). Does this passage from Zechariah also echo the gate liturgies? Is that why Matthew says that it is fulfilled as Jesus comes to the gates of Jerusalem?

Zec 9:10, the continuation of the verse quoted by Matthew, clearly echoes Ps 2:7-9 and contrasts with it. This echo will become audible to us if we first give our attention to Psalm 2, and then compare it with Zec 9:10.

Psalm 2 is a royal enthronement psalm. When a king came into his inheritance he would pass through the gates of Jerusalem as part of the enthronement ceremony. Psalm 2 and other scripture passages give us an idea of what the enthronement liturgy was like. Solomon, for example, was anointed king outside the city walls at the fountain of Gihon in the Kedron Valley. Then he was escorted up to the city in a joyous procession with music and acclamation, and enthroned in David's palace (1 Kgs 1:33-40).

At his birth, Solomon had been named by Yahweh: *Jedidiah*, "Beloved of Yahweh." "The Lord loved him and sent the prophet Nathan to name him Jedidiah on behalf of the Lord" (2 Sm 12:24-25, n). This new name signified Solomon's election by Yahweh to fulfill Yahweh's purposes in accord with his covenant with David. The story of Solomon's enthronement in spite of Adonijah's plot to seize the throne (1 Kgs 1:1-32) shows that human plotting cannot frustrate the purposes of Yahweh, who chooses his "Beloved" to accomplish his purposes. This idea is also clearly expressed in Psalm 2:

Why this tumult among nations,
among peoples this useless murmuring?
They arise, the kings of the earth,
princes plot against the Lord and his Anointed.
"Come, let us break their fetters,
come, let us cast off their yoke."

He who sits in the heavens laughs;
the Lord is laughing them to scorn.
Then he will speak in his anger,
his rage will strike them with terror.
"It is I who have set up my king
on Zion, my holy mountain"
(Ps 2:1-6, g).

The idea is still more clearly elaborated in Acts 4:23-31, which quotes this psalm. The psalmist points out that God uses schemes against the Lord and his Messiah to accomplish

what he, in his powerful providence, planned long ago (Acts
4:28). Nothing can frustrate God's loving purposes.

At his anointing, a new king was given a divine decree,
declaring his authority to rule. The king proclaims this decree
from his throne:

> I will announce the decree of the Lord:
> The Lord said to me: "You are my Son.
> It is I who have begotten you this day.
> Ask and I shall bequeath you the nations,
> put the ends of the earth in your possession.
> With a rod of iron you will break them,
> shatter them like a potter's jar"
> > (Ps 2:7-9, g).

Then the new king issues an ultimatum to the kings of the
earth:

> Now, O kings, understand,
> take warning, rulers of the earth;
> serve the Lord with awe
> and trembling, pay him your homage
> lest he be angry and you perish;
> for suddenly his anger will blaze
> > (Ps 2:10-11, g).

At their enthronement, Judah's kings were given throne
names, expressing the role they were to fulfill and their au-
thorization to act in God's name. Emmanuel's throne names,
for example, were "Wonderful Counselor," "Mighty God,"
"Everlasting Father," "Prince of Peace" (Is 9:6, r). Jedidiah's
throne name was "Solomon," signifying his task of bringing
peace and security to his people through the wise administra-
tion of justice. "Solomon," (peaceful) derives from *shalom*
which signifies the blessing of God's covenant with his people.

Solomon was Jedidiah, "Beloved of Yahweh." Jesus is the
Beloved Son, chosen to fulfill what Solomon had only fore-
shadowed. When Jesus enters the royal city of David as Son of

David, Messianic King, he comes from the Mount of Olives, the source of the oil used in ceremonies of anointing. Gethsemane, the garden on the Mount of Olives, means "oil press." Jesus crosses the Kedron Valley where Solomon had been anointed king. He passes through the gates and enters the temple, joyously acclaimed by the people just as Solomon was. He asserts his royal messianic authority in the temple saying, "My house shall be called a house of prayer!" (Mt 21:13, n). His statement corresponds to the king's ultimatum in Psalm 2.

Yet Jesus is not enthroned as Messianic King on this occasion. He is the stone rejected by the builders, which at the resurrection becomes the cornerstone of the new edifice. He does not proclaim the decree granting him divine authority on that day of his triumphant entry into Jerusalem. That decree is proclaimed only after his resurrection, which is his true enthronement: "Full authority has been given to me both in heaven and on earth" (Mt 28:18, n).

The ultimatum in Ps 2:7-11 contains a warlike threat. Zec 9:10 clearly echoes Psalm 2 but adds a new twist: "He shall proclaim peace to the nations," he says of the Messianic King. The Lord's Anointed in Psalm 2 is authorized to shatter the nations like a potter's jar (2:9). Not only will Zechariah's Messianic King establish peace within Israel, reuniting the northern and southern kingdoms like a new Solomon ("He shall banish the chariot from Ephraim and the horse from Jerusalem"), but "He shall proclaim peace to the nations . . . to the ends of the earth" (Zec 9:10, n).

When Matthew tells us that Jesus came into Jerusalem riding an ass, he is saying that Jesus fulfills the prophecy of Zec 9:9-10. Though Matthew shows that Jesus is acclaimed the Son of David (21:9), he corrects the wrong impression given by the warlike imagery of Psalm 2. He does this by presenting Jesus as the peaceful king described by Zechariah, and, in so doing, he profoundly modifies the meaning of king.

Zechariah describes the king as "meek, humble" (*ani*). He adds a new aspect to the portrait of the coming Messiah. It is the same characteristic that Zephaniah attributes to the just and holy people of the future: "I will leave as a remnant in

your midst a people humble *ani* and lowly, who shall take
refuge in the name of the Lord" (Zep 3:12). Jesus describes
these people in his eight beatitudes (Mt 5:3-12).

Compare Zep 3:11-17 with Zec 9:9-10. In the first passage,
Daughter Zion is invited to rejoice in the presence of Yahweh,
her King. In the second, she is invited to rejoice in the coming
of the Messiah, her King.

> Shout for joy, O daughter Zion. . . .
> Be glad and exalt with all your heart,
>   O daughter Jerusalem!. . .
> The king of Israel, the Lord,
>   is in your midst . . .
> The Lord, your God, is in your midst,
>   a mighty savior;
> He will rejoice over you with gladness,
>   and renew you in his love,
> He will sing joyfully because of you,
>   as one sings at festivals
>   (Zep 3:14-17, n).

> Rejoice heartily, O daughter Zion,
> shout for joy, O daughter Jerusalem!
> See, your king shall come to you;
> a just savior is he,
> Meek, and riding on an ass. . .
> and he shall proclaim peace to the nations
>   (Zec 9:9-10, n).

Matthew's words, "Tell the daughter of Zion" (21:5), gather
together not only Isaiah 62 and its message, but also Zep
3:14-17 and Zec 9:9-10 and their messages. All these messages
are fulfilled in the coming of Jesus, who is both God and
Messiah.

Be Humble

The spirituality of the *anawim*, Zephaniah's poor and humble
who trust only in Yahweh (Zep 3:12), is the spirituality of

Jesus, meek and humble of heart: "Learn from me, for I am gentle and humble of heart" (Mt 11:29, n). The only kind of messianic claim that Jesus publicly professed was the claim to be the Messiah who was one of God's lowly and humble people. He proclaims this, not in word, but in deed, entering the royal city on a lowly ass. He fulfills the spiritual ideal of Israel by living it himself as the true Israel. He practices what he preaches in the eight beatitudes.

Zechariah's phrase, "riding on an ass," indicates the peaceful intent of the Messianic King. Jesus comes, riding, not a horse, symbol of the conqueror, but the ass, work beast of the poor (Gn 49:11). The ass was used for peaceful, friendly entry, the horse was the mount for war. Solomon, "the Peaceful," wanting no war with Adonijah, rode a mule, not a warhorse, on the day of his anointing (1 Kgs 1:33-34). "But you have a greater than Solomon here!" (Mt 12:42, n).

Jesus is not like those proud successors of David who trusted in horses and chariots rather than in the Lord (Is 30:15-18; Jer 17:25). "Some are strong in chariots; some in horses; but we are strong in the name of the Lord our God!" (Ps 20:8, n). This psalm is a prayer for the king, who is to trust not in armaments, but in Yahweh's Name. Yahweh's Name signified his presence and power. "Blessed is he who comes in the name of the Lord" means "comes trusting in the Lord." Jesus fulfills Zephaniah's description of the true Israel: "a people humble and lowly, who shall take refuge in the name of the Lord" (Zep 3:12, n). Jesus teaches this attitude to his disciples in the eight beatitudes and by his whole life.

TWELVE

Judgment Upon the "Den of Thieves"

Matthew's chapters 21-23 are an inclusion between the twice repeated verse from Psalm 118: "Blessed is he who comes in the name of the Lord." The verse is quoted initially in reference to Christ's first coming (Mt 21:9), and then in reference to his final coming as judge (23:39). It holds a precious clue to the deeper interpretation of the contents of these three chapters.

Rejected at his first coming, Jesus predicts that God will abandon the temple until the people acclaim Jesus at the final coming, saying, "Blessed is he who comes in the name of the Lord" (23:39). Even at the first coming, Jerusalem seems to have had some sort of premonition of his coming as judge. Matthew hints at this, we have seen, by saying that the city is shaken as if by an earthquake when Jesus enters. This meek and humble King of Peace, now riding on an ass, will later be seen "coming on the clouds of heaven with great power and glory" (Mt 24:30, n).

To "come in the name of the Lord" is to come as a presence of God, endowed with God's power and authority. In the first scene of the inclusion (Mt 21:12-13), Jesus enters the temple as the Anointed King. This is no ordinary liturgy at the gate. It is not just a procession of pilgrims to the temple on a feast day. It is an enthronement procession. The Messianic King comes to proclaim his authority. He exercises his messianic authority in the temple by cleansing it of buyers and sellers. His words as he does this are like a proclamation of the divine decree establishing him as king: "My house shall be called a house of prayer, but you are turning it into a den of thieves" (Mt 21:13, n).

These are words from Is 56:7 and Jer 7:11. They reveal Jesus' intention when he performs the prophetic action of clearing the temple. They show how he understood his mission.

The cleansing of the temple symbolizes Jesus' coming judgment upon Jerusalem. Notice that he quotes Jeremiah when he says that the temple was turning into a "den of thieves" (Jer 7:1-15). These words from the Old Testament prophet must be considered in their total context. They occur in a scene of judgment upon Jerusalem. It is possible that the scene took place during a liturgy at the gate. Jeremiah addresses "all you who enter these gates to worship the Lord" (Jer 7:2). Only the just may pass through the gates of justice, and Jeremiah pronounces judgment upon those who are entering. Clearly, their lives have been characterized by unrighteousness and injustice.

> Only if you thoroughly reform your ways and your deeds; if each of you deals justly with his neighbor; if you no longer oppress the resident alien, the orphan, and the widow; if you no longer shed innocent blood in this place, or follow strange gods to your own harm, will I remain with you in this place, in the land which I gave to your fathers long ago and forever (Jer 7:5-7, n).

The people have come to the temple to enjoy God's presence and friendship. But if they do not repent, they will not find him there. "Reform your ways and your deeds, so that I may remain with you in this place" (7:3). Though it is "the temple of the Lord" (7:4), "the house which bears my name" (7-10) (i.e., consecrated as the place of his special presence), "the dwelling place of his name" (7:12), he will not remain there if they remain in their injustice. They must not say, "We are safe" (7:10), for only the righteous are safe (Ps 15:5).

Though Jer 7:1-11 issues a call to conversion, the rest of the passage (12-15) pronounces judgment upon a people too obstinate to listen. God will destroy the Jerusalem temple just as he destroyed his dwelling place at Shiloh:

Has this house which bears my name become in your eyes a den of thieves? I too see what is being done, says the Lord. You may go to Shiloh, which I made the dwelling place of my name in the beginning. See what I did to it because of the wickedness of my people Israel. And now because you have committed all these misdeeds, says the Lord, because you did not listen, though I spoke to you untiringly; because you did not answer, though I called you, I will do to this house named after me, in which you trust, and to this place which I gave to you and your fathers, just as I did to Shiloh. I will cast you away from me, as I cast away all your brethren, all the offspring of Ephraim (Jer 7:11-15, n).

By repeating "den of thieves" from Jeremiah's proclamation of divine judgment upon Jerusalem, Jesus interprets his own action in cleansing the temple. It is a symbol of coming judgment upon the people of his own times. Symbolically, Jesus drives from God's presence all those guilty of injustice. Like Jeremiah's words, Jesus' words and actions are first of all a call to conversion. But when he and his message are rejected, Jesus leaves the temple for the last time, pronouncing judgment upon those who refuse to accept him:

Recall the saying, 'You will find your temple deserted.' I tell you, you will not see me from this time on until you declare, 'Blessed is he who comes in the name of the Lord' (Mt 23:38-39, n).

This reference to his final coming leads into our Lord's great eschatological discourse, which follows immediately (Mt 24:1-26:1). In this discourse, the judgment upon Jerusalem becomes a warning to all mankind. Jerusalem's destruction forecasts judgment upon all the unrepentant, all who reject Christ the Savior. That is why, in the eschatological discourse, Matthew blends his account of the destruction of Jerusalem with his account of the final coming of the Lord as judge. The judgment upon Jerusalem is a first symptom of the judgment upon all mankind.

Readers of Matthew's gospel should understand that everything Jesus says and does in his first coming is a call to conversion. Much of the message included between the two references to his coming, "Blessed is he who comes in the name of
the Lord," contains a challenge to conversion, to acceptance of
the Savior-Messiah. Only through conversion could Jerusalem
escape the judgment of which she had a premonition when
Jesus entered the city. The same is true for us all. The mere fact
that there is a call to conversion implies that even here and
now, in the first coming of Jesus, we are under God's ever-
present judgment. We are invited to escape condemnation by
accepting the peaceable, humble Savior who is unwilling to
crush the bruised reed (Mt 12:20).

A Warning and a Hope

Jesus' parting words as he leaves the temple for the last time
before his passion are not words of final judgment upon Jerusalem. They are words of warning and of hope.

He warns the people with the words, "Recall the saying,
'You will find your temple deserted'" (Mt 23:38, n). His words
allude to Jer 12:7, where Yahweh says, "I will abandon my
house, cast off my heritage; the beloved of my soul I deliver
into the hands of her foes." The fact that God abandoned the
temple to the Babylonians in Jeremiah's day should be a warning to the Jerusalem of Jesus' day and a warning to the readers
of Matthew in every age.

Jesus follows these words of warning with words of hope:
"I tell you, you will not see me from this time on until you
declare, 'Blessed is he who comes in the name of the Lord'"
(23:39, n). Jesus has finished his preaching to Jerusalem. They
will see him no more as a preacher on earth. But he leaves
the door open to faith and repentance. The moment the
people welcome him into their hearts in faith and accept him
as Messiah, saying, "Blessed is he who comes in the name of
the Lord," Jesus will be present with them as risen Lord. Any
time they turn to him, they will find him; they do not have to
wait for his coming at the last judgment. He comes in the

For my house shall be called
  a house of prayer for all peoples.
Thus says the Lord God, who gathers the dispersed of
  Israel:
Others will I gather to him
  besides those already gathered
                    (Is 56:7-8, n).

Though the phrase "others will I gather" may have referred
simply to the return of still more of the dispersed of Israel, its
obscurity permits "the others" to refer to the nations. Thus it
confirms the preceding lines, "The foreigners . . . I will bring to
my holy mountain and make joyful in my house of prayer. . . .
For my house shall be called a house of prayer for all peoples"
(Is 56:6-7, n).

One may wonder why Matthew omits "for all peoples"
when Jesus quotes this last sentence in the temple. Mark does
not omit those words when he reports this same event (Mk
11:17; Mt 21:13). It would seem that keeping the words "for all
peoples" would have strengthened Matthew's thesis that Jesus
"proclaims justice to the Gentiles . . . and in his name will the
Gentiles hope" (Mt 12:18, 21, r). Because Jesus "fulfills all righteousness" (Mt 3:15), God brings the nations to his holy mountain (Is 56:7).

Matthew omits "for all peoples" because the nations shall
not come to this temple of stone in Jerusalem, which soon will
be destroyed by the Romans. They shall come to the eschatological temple built upon Jesus, the rejected stone that becomes
the keystone of the living temple, the body of Christ. The
worship of the true God is to be communicated to all peoples
through Jesus, the rejected but risen Messiah, and not through
the temple of Jerusalem.

Therefore only at the end of this twenty-first chapter does
Jesus speak of the ingathering of the harvest of the nations.
The chapter is an inclusion, we said, between two references to
Psalm 118, "Blessed is he who comes" (21:9) and "The stone
which the builders rejected" (21:42, n). At the beginning of the
chapter, as he comes into the temple, Matthew's Jesus says

simply, "My house shall be called a house of prayer," and omits the words, "for all the peoples." Then in the course of the inclusion, Jesus tells the parable of the vinedressers who reject and murder the owner's son (21:33-43). He then applies to himself the words of the psalm, "The stone which the builders rejected has become the keystone of the structure. It was the Lord who did this, and we find it marvelous to behold" (21:42, n). Only then does he speak of the ingathering of the harvest of the nations: "For this reason, I tell you, the kingdom of God will be taken away from you and given to a nation that will yield a rich harvest" (21:43, n).

Psalm 118, with its reference to the rejected stone, was a harvest thanksgiving psalm. It was used at the Feast of Tabernacles, celebrating the ingathering of the grape and olive harvests. Because Jesus' own people reject him, the kingdom of God is taken from them and given to a nation gathered in from all the peoples of the world, including Jews who do accept Jesus as Messiah.

The peoples of the earth are gathered, not into the old temple built of stone, but into the living house of God built upon the risen Jesus, the living stone. Only Jesus fulfills the words of Isaiah, "My house shall be called a house of prayer for all peoples" (Is 56:7, n).

By proclaiming these words as he enters the temple, Jesus is announcing that he has come to gather the peoples into God's living house of prayer. But he comes, not on the Feast of Tabernacles—the feast of the ingathering of the harvest—though he is welcomed with waving green branches, a ceremony typical of this feast. He comes on the Feast of Passover. For it is only through his own sacrifice as the Paschal Lamb that he gathers the peoples in his blood. Only his death and resurrection make possible this ingathering of the nations. Jesus forbade preaching to the pagans before his death and resurrection. "My mission is only to the lost sheep of the house of Israel" (Mt 15:24, n). "Do not visit pagan territory and do not enter a Samaritan town. Go instead after the lost sheep of the house of Israel" (Mt 10:6, n).

But when he is enthroned at God's right hand after his

death and resurrection, he proclaims the divine decree establishing his kingship: "All authority in heaven and on earth
has been given to me" (Mt 28:18, r). Only then does he
commission his disciples to gather together the nations into
the community worshipping the One God: "Go therefore
and make disciples of all nations, baptizing them in the
name of the Father and of the Son and of the Holy Spirit"
(Mt 28:19, r).

The Blind and the Lame Cured in the Temple

Not only will the house of prayer be opened to all peoples,
but it will receive the blind, the lame, the castrated, the despised, the outcast—all who have been excluded from the
temple. For the eunuchs along with the foreigners, says Isaiah,
will be admitted to the Lord's house of prayer. Jesus has come
to put this word of Isaiah into full effect, and he proclaims this
in the words of the prophet: "My house shall be called a house
of prayer" (Mt 21:13, n).

Therefore Matthew's next words are profoundly significant.
"The blind and the lame came to him inside the temple area
and he cured them" (Mt 21:14, n). Traditionally those who
were maimed, crippled, or blind were excluded from the
temple. The fact that these handicapped persons had entered
the sacred precincts was contrary to all custom and revolting to
the leaders of worship: "The chief priests and the scribes became indignant when they observed the wonders he worked,
and how the children were shouting out in the temple precincts, 'Hosanna to the Son of David!'" (Mt 21:15, n). They
were probably so angry with the outcasts who came in with
Jesus that they could not see the miracles of healing that qualified them to be there. All the outcasts and the miserable are
called by Jesus to the wholeness of salvation and into the very
presence of God (Mt 11:5).

As he heals the blind and the lame in the temple, the children acclaim him anew as Messiah: "Hosanna to the Son of
David!" (Mt 21:15). Jesus, Son of David, loves the blind and the
lame, whereas an old proverb claimed that David hated them:

Then the king and his men set out for Jerusalem against the Jebusites who inhabited the region. David was told, "You cannot enter here: the blind and the lame will drive you away!" which was their way of saying, "David cannot enter here." But David did take the stronghold of Zion, which is the City of David. On that day David said: "All who wish to attack the Jebusites must strike at them through the water shaft. The lame and the blind shall be the personal enemies of David." That is why it is said, "The blind and the lame shall not enter the palace" (2 Sm 5:6-9, n).

The word here translated as "palace" is also the word for "house," and could mean God's house, rather than David's palace. Possibly this story was told to justify the exclusion of the handicapped from the temple. But what did the story really mean? "The blind and the lame will drive you away!" That is, the fortress is so strong that the handicapped are the only defenders it needs. This is typical Semitic language expressed in riddles. David answers in kind: "The blind and the lame shall be the personal enemies of David." This merely means, "I will conquer this impregnable fortress, I will defeat its 'blind' and 'lame' defenders." But he does not take the city by force. His men sneak in through the water tunnel leading up from the spring of Gihon.

Those who interpret everything in scripture in terms of typology might infer from this incident that we enter the New Jerusalem through the tunnel pierced into the Rock, the side of Jesus Crucified, from which pours forth the living waters springing up to eternal life.

As Jesus enters the royal city, which David won when he conquered the Jebusites, he receives the blind and the lame lovingly and heals them. Rightly the children acclaim, "Hosanna to the Son of David!"

With these words, Psalm 118 surfaces again. "Hosanna!" means, "Grant salvation." In the psalm, "Hosanna" is addressed to Yahweh: "O Lord, grant salvation!" In Matthew, chapter 21, it is addressed to Jesus, "Hosanna to the Son of David!"

The Son of God

"The chief priests and the scribes became indignant when they observed the wonders he worked, and how the children were shouting out in the temple precincts, 'Hosanna to the Son of David!'" (Mt 21:15, n). Through the wonders Jesus worked, the healing of the blind and the lame, salvation breaks into the world. These are signs that the saving God is present in power. The priests and scribes are blind to the meaning of these signs, but the children get the point. Their shouts of acclamation are the only appropriate response. Their words, "Hosanna, grant salvation," imply that Jesus is the Savior. They acclaim him as Savior by asking him to put his saving power to work.

Jesus accepts the acclamations of the children, though the priests and scribes pressure him to repudiate them. "Do you hear what they are saying?" the priests ask. "Of course!" says Jesus. And I approve of what they are saying. You would know they are expressing the truth if you knew your Scriptures as well as you claim. "Did you never read, 'From the mouth of babes and nurslings Thou hast perfected praise?'" (Mt 21:16, m).

The children who acclaim Jesus in the temple symbolize "the little ones" of all Christian generations. "Little ones" is another of the threads woven through Matthew's tapestry. The revelation of the Father and the Son, "hidden from the learned and clever" priests and scribes, is "revealed to the merest children" (Mt 11:25, n). In Matthew's Greek "merest children," *nepioi*, is the same word used in the phrase "from the mouth of babes" (21:16). All the disciples must become like little children (Mt 18:3). Though they are despised and rejected by men (Mt 19:13, 15), they are received by Jesus, and he is recognized by them. Were some of those children who acclaimed Jesus in the temple among those whom he received and blessed when the disciples tried to send them away (Mt 19:13)?

"The little ones" represent all true believers, the disciples of Jesus in every age, even to the end of time. The eight beatitudes perfectly describe them. They are "the poor of Yahweh." Their cry, "Hosanna!," will be on the lips of Christians till the end of time as they acclaim their Savior.

When they cry out to Jesus in the temple, the children are continuing the acclamation with which the crowds greeted Jesus at the city gates: "Hosanna to the Son of David! Blessed is he who comes in the name of the Lord" (Mt 21:9). Even so, the crowd and the children have only limited insight into Jesus. Their words of acclamation only foreshadow the more perfect acclaim they will be able to offer Jesus when he is enthroned in his resurrection.

Here they say to him, "Blessed is he who comes in the name of the Lord." "The name" signifies the presence and power of Yahweh himself. It is yet another theme, a thread running through Matthew's tapestry, e.g., "You are to name him Jesus, because he will save his people from their sins. . . . They shall call him Emmanuel, a name which means 'God is with us'" (Mt 1:21, 23); "In his name, the Gentiles will find hope" (Mt 12:21, n).

Here, the Son of David comes in the name of the Lord, i.e., endowed with Yahweh's power and authority. To welcome Jesus as one endowed with God's power does not necessarily mean that the people already see that he is God. Though they greet him as the One who comes in the name of the Lord, they can still ask about him, "Who is this?" (Mt 21:10), and the suggested answer is "This is the Prophet" (21:11). But he is infinitely more than a prophet. The very fact that the people question who it is that has been acclaimed the Son of David— "Who is this?"—implies that he is much more than a human son of David.

Jesus helps them to understand who he is by means of various incidents narrated within the inclusion that opens and closes with the acclamation, "Blessed is he who comes in the name of the Lord."

"Jesus put a question to the assembled Pharisees" (Mt 22:41, n). The word "assembled" echoes Psalm 2, in which the nations and their rulers assembled against the Lord and his Messiah. It also echoes the story of the Magi, in which Herod assembles the priests and scribes, and plots against Jesus.

Jesus put a question to the assembled Pharisees, "What is your opinion about the Messiah? Whose son is he?"

"David's," they answered. He said to them, "Then how is it that David under the Spirit's influence calls him 'lord,' as he does: 'The Lord said to my lord, Sit at my right hand, until I humble your enemies beneath your feet?' If David calls him 'lord,' how can he be his son? (Mt 22:41-45, n).

Thus Jesus points the enquiring minds of the people towards his coming enthronement at God's right hand. He points the high priest in the same direction: "I tell you this: Soon you will see the Son of Man seated at the right hand of the Power and coming on the clouds of heaven" (Mt 26:64, n).

Full Authority

Though Jesus' entrance into Jerusalem on Palm Sunday is like a royal enthronement procession, the enthronement does not actually take place at that time. Jesus is rejected by his people. "The stone which the builders rejected has become the keystone of the structure" (Mt 21:42, n). Only in his resurrection is he enthroned at God's right hand. The true enthronement scene takes place in the closing scene of Matthew's gospel. Here Jesus, like the anointed king in Psalm 2, proclaims the divine decree authorizing his reign: "Full authority has been given to me both in heaven and on earth" (Mt 28:18, n).

Thus the children's acclamations in the temple, "Hosanna to the Son of David," anticipate and symbolize the perfect praise given to Jesus when he is enthroned in his death and resurrection. The risen Jesus is Lord not only of Jerusalem, the city of David, but of the whole universe. "Full authority both in heaven and on earth has been given to me." To this King all Christian generations cry, "Hosanna!"

Jesus hints at this perfect praise when he reminds the chief priests and the scribes of Psalm 8, "Did you never read, 'From the mouth of babes and nurslings Thou hast perfected praise?'" (Mt 21:16, m). He quotes the verse, not from the Hebrew, but from the Septuagint, the Greek version of the psalm. The Greek reads, "From the mouth of babes and nurslings Thou hast perfected *praise*," and the Hebrew reads, "By the mouth of babes and infants, thou hast founded a *bulwark* because of thy foes, to still the enemy and the avenger" (Ps 8:2, r).

The Greek text is not false to the Hebrew original but interprets it correctly. The praise formed by God in the mouths of infants becomes a fortress against God's enemies. This praise comes in response to the Name and Majesty of God, which are manifest in the glory of the heavens and of the earth: "O Lord, our Lord, how glorious is your *name* over all the earth! You have exalted your *majesty* above the heavens" (Ps 8:2, n).

"Name" and "majesty" are synonymous with God himself, who is exalted above all that he has made. God is present and manifest in his "name" and "glory." In response to this manifestation, the little ones glorify his name. This praise of his name in their mouths is a mighty power restraining and silencing the enemies of God: "Out of the mouths of babes and sucklings you have fashioned praise because of your foes, to silence the hostile and the vengeful" (Ps 8:3, n).

The Hebrew reads: You have fashioned "strength" (k, m) "out of the mouths of babes." The revelation of the true God and the acceptance of his name in true faith gives impregnable power and strength even to the smallest and weakest disciple. When the name of the Lord is in our hearts and on our lips, the rebellious adversaries of God are confounded and silenced. "The name of the Lord is a strong tower; the just man runs to it and is safe" (Pv 18:10, n).

The chief priests and scribes, the adversaries assembled against Jesus, are silenced by the praise of the children in the temple (Mt 21:15-16). For they are already under judgment; the "earthquake" that stirs them as Jesus comes into the city is a premonition of this. Those who witness against them are "the little ones" who have confessed the name of the Lord Jesus; just as Herod the Great is confounded by the witness of the innocent infants whom he murdered in Bethlehem.

These children, in turn, symbolize all "the little ones," the disciples of Jesus whose witness to the name confounds their persecutors. For the rulers and kings of the earth are assembled together against the disciples whom Jesus sends to preach. This is suggested by the word "synagogue," which comes from the Greek word for "assemble."

> They will hale you into the court,
>   they will flog you in their synagogues.
> You will be brought to trial before rulers and kings
>   to give witness before them and before the Gentiles
> on my account. . . .
> Whoever acknowledges me before men
>   I will acknowledge before my Father in heaven.
>   (Mt 10:17-18, 32, n)

The nations and their rulers assemble against the disciples just as they did against Jesus himself. "No pupil outranks his teacher, no slave his master. The pupil should be glad to become like his teacher, the slave like his master" (Mt 10:24-25, n). The disciple follows the Lord into the storm at sea. The Lord calms the sea by the power of his word. The disciple silences the adversaries by the power of praise, the praise of the name of Jesus. His name contains power to confound and silence the enemy.

In Psalm 8, the Lord's name (Yahweh's name) is exalted above both the heavens and the earth. This is now verified also in Jesus, to whom all authority in heaven and on earth is given (Mt 28:18). Psalm 8 can now be addressed directly to Jesus.

When Jesus says that the children's acclamation of praise, "Hosanna to the Son of David," fulfills this psalm, he is pointing, we said, to the fully enlightened praise that will be his when he is enthroned in his resurrection and all things are subjected to him. The children's witness prefigures the Christian witness which proclaims that in Jesus man's dominion over the created universe, usurped by Satan, has been restored.

Psalm 8 speaks of the eminent dignity of mankind before God:

> When I behold your heavens, the work of your fingers,
>   the moon and the stars which you set in place

What is man that you should be mindful of him,
   or the son of man that you should care for him?

You have made him little less than the angels,
   and crowned him with glory and honor.
You have given him rule over the works of your hands,
   putting all things under his feet
               (Ps 8:4-7, n).

When Jesus is exalted at the right hand of God and all things
are subjected to him, this psalm is fulfilled. Yet its fulfillment
greatly surpasses the dominion of which the psalm was speaking. In the psalm, man is made master only of the created
universe. Jesus, the perfect man, is master of the new creation
as well.

Since Psalm 8 echoes the creation story in Genesis, we can
assume that Satan and his seed are the enemies of which it
speaks, the adversaries silenced by praise from the mouths of
infants (Gn 3:15). When Jesus' name is exalted over all the
earth and his majesty is extolled in the heavens, when the
praise of this name is formed in the mouths of the little ones by
the Holy Spirit, then the adversaries are silenced. The children's witness in the temple, though it acclaims Jesus merely
as Messiah, the Son of David, prefigures the perfect praise that
will be given him by his disciples, when he is enthroned as
Lord of all the heavens and the earth.

Perfect Praise

But there is even more to that perfect praise. The little ones
who acclaim Jesus as Son of David will see him not simply as
the perfect man, lord of all creation, in whose person dominion
over creation has been restored to mankind. Above all, they
will see him as very Son of the Father, and their perfect praise
will share in the Son's own praise:

Father, Lord of heaven and earth, to you I offer praise; for
what you have hidden from the learned and the clever you
have revealed to the merest children. Father, it is true. You

have graciously willed it so. Everything has been given over to me by my Father. No one knows the Son but the Father, and no one knows the Father but the Son - and anyone to whom the Son wishes to reveal him (Mt 11:25-27, n).

The "merest children" are the disciples of Jesus to whom is revealed the mystery known by no one except the Father and the Son: the secrets of the inner life of God, the wonders of the Father, Son, and Holy Spirit.

He to whom all authority in heaven and on earth has been given empowers his missionaries to bring all the nations into this mystery:

Go, therefore, and make disciples of all the nations.
Baptize them in the Name
   of the Father
   and the Son
   and of the Holy Spirit (Mt 28:19, n).

"O Lord, our Lord, how glorious is your name over all the earth!" (Ps 8:2, 10).

FOURTEEN

Glory and Victory in the House of God

In our opening chapter, we interpreted Jesus' entry into Jerusalem on Palm Sunday in light of the prophet Haggai. This interpretation is justified for several reasons.

Haggai speaks of the earthshaking events accomplished by the Lord. Matthew presents Jesus' entry into the city as earthshaking. The rebuilding of the temple after the Babylonian Exile is the focus of the Book of Haggai, just as the temple is the focus in Matthew, chapter 21. This chapter consists of an inclusion between two references to Psalm 118. The closing reference, "The stone which the builders rejected has become the keystone of the structure" (Ps 118:22; Mt 21:42, n), originally referred, no doubt, to the rebuilding of the temple after the return from Babylon. Haggai urges the people to perform the task of rebuilding.

According to Haggai, the shaking of the whole world and the rebuilding of the temple will inaugurate the messianic era. When God shakes the world, all its treasures will come flowing in to give glory to the temple (Hg 2:6-9). When God shakes the world and crushes its kingdoms, the Son of David, God's signet ring, will rule as Messiah (Hg 2:20-23).

When Matthew says that Jerusalem was shaken as if by an earthquake as Jesus enters the city, he is saying that these prophecies are being fulfilled by Jesus.

In Haggai's time, an age of crop failures and great economic hardship, the people were so preoccupied with their own worries that they neglected the worship of God. It is "not yet the time" for rebuilding the temple, they said (Hg 1:2). The prophet tells them that their neglect of God and their failure to rebuild the place of worship has caused their blessings to dry up (Hg 1:1-15). He promises immediate blessings from the moment that they lay the foundations for the new temple (Hg 2:15-19). Neglect of the worship of God can only mean disaster for mankind. Obviously Haggai is fully relevant in our day when atheism and secularism are so prevalent. The earthshaking disasters of our times will be replaced with blessings only when modern man returns to having reverence for God and for the order he has established.

One month after beginning work on the foundations of the temple, Haggai admits the unspoken discouragement of the older people who had seen the glory of Solomon's temple. By contrast, the new temple seems like nothing:

> Who is left among you that saw this house in its former glory? And how do you see it now? Does it not seem like nothing in your eyes? But now take courage . . . says the Lord . . . and work! For I am with you, says the Lord of hosts. . . . I will shake the heavens and the earth. . . . and I will fill this house with glory, says the Lord of hosts. . . . Greater will be the future glory of this house than the former (Hg 2:3-9, n).

The prophet is calling the people to a great act of faith, expressed by their courageous work of rebuilding the temple. He is telling them that God is about to do something world-shaking. By their faith and work they must prepare the way.

The glory of God's action will be all the more manifest considering what he has to work with. The people are a poor, bedraggled "remnant" (1:12, 14; 2:2). A "remnant" was what remained of a people in the aftermath of a war that aimed at their total destruction. They find themselves in an utterly discouraging condition of poverty and crop failure. And the building they are putting up in place of the glorious temple of Solomon is disappointingly inglorious.

Haggai fires their faith and courage by proclaiming the word of the Lord: "I am with you, says the Lord" (1:13; 2:4). The Lord himself "stirred up the spirit" of the governor, the high priest, and "the spirit of all the remnant of the people" (Hg 1:14, n). The Spirit of the Lord is at work with them! "My spirit continues in your midst; do not fear!" (2:5, n).

They are to trust in God's faithfulness to the covenant that he made with them when he brought them out of Egypt centuries before. "For I am with you, says the Lord of hosts. This is the pact that I made with you when you came out of Egypt, and my spirit continues in your midst; do not fear" (Hg 2:4-5, n). In other words, God stipulated in his covenant with Israel that he would always be with them; the power of his own spirit would work in them. This is the source of their courage: "Take courage, all you people of the land, and work!" (2:4).

In other words, salvation history is not over. God's words, "I am with you!" had always been addressed to the charismatic leaders he had raised up as instruments of his saving work (e.g., Ex 3:12; Jer 1:6-8; Jgs 6:12-16; Jos 1:5-9; Is 41:10; 43:2; Lk 1:28-30; Ps 46). "I am with you" is also the great theme of Matthew's ecclesial gospel. The whole gospel is an inclusion, we have seen, between two references to Emmanuel, God-with-us: "You are to name him Jesus. . . . and they shall call him Emmanuel, a name which means, 'God is with us'" (Mt 1:21, 23, n) and "Know that I am with you always, until the end of the world!" (Mt 28:20, n).

Matthew's brief allusion to Haggai's prophecy about God acting to shake the heavens and the earth means that God is about to take earthshaking action through Jesus, his signet ring (Mt 21:10). Salvation history is not over!

Small Beginnings

Out of "small beginnings" (Zec 4:10), God is going to do something greater than ever. He is about to shake the whole creation. The people and their leaders must prepare for this event and place themselves at Yahweh's disposal by rebuilding the temple. The temple is to be the focal point for their faith. Prepare the temple for the coming of the Lord!

Zechariah, Haggai's immediate successor, continues the same trend of thought:

> This is the Lord's message to Zerubbabel: Not by an army, nor by might, but by my spirit, says the Lord of hosts. What are you, O great mountain? Before Zerubbabel you are but a plain. He shall bring out the capstone amid exclamations of 'Hail, Hail' to it (Zec 4:6-7, n).

We think of the hosannas that we address to the risen Jesus, the rejected stone which has become the keystone.

> This word of the Lord then came to me: The hands of Zerubbabel have laid the foundations of this house, and his hands shall finish it; then you shall know that the Lord of hosts has sent me to you. For even they who were scornful on that day of small beginnings shall rejoice to see the select stone in the hands of Zerubbabel (Zec 4:8-10, n).

Mountainous obstacles will be overcome (4:7). "Small beginnings" (4:10) will be completed in great glory, but "not by an army, nor by might, but by my spirit, says the Lord of hosts" (4:6).

The small beginnings at Zerubbabel's disposal referred not merely to the disappointingly inglorious temple he was building and not merely to the city of Jerusalem, which was still largely a heap of rubble after the destruction by the Babylonians. Above all, the small beginnings were the people, the poverty-striken remnant who had returned from Exile.

In Matthew, the small beginnings are found in the person of the meek and lowly Jesus, who comes in humility riding on an ass, the rejected stone who becomes the select stone, the keystone of the whole structure. "The stone which the builders rejected has become the keystone of the structure" (Mt 21:42). These words take the form of a proverb. They mean that a radical change is brought about, a great reversal of human plans and projects. Those who reject Jesus and plot his death unwittingly prepare the way for his glory.

Matthew's gospel, throughout, is a gospel of "small beginnings." The poor in spirit receive the kingdom (5:3). The poor have the gospel preached to them (11:5). The kingdom of God is like a tiny mustard seed, "the smallest seed of all," which becomes a great tree (13:32). The remnant—the despised, the outcast, the blind, and the lame—are admitted to God's friendship. To the merest children the deepest mysteries of God are revealed (11:25). The whole of Matthew's gospel can be read as a commentary on the eight beatitudes. The poor of Yahweh receive the blessings of the Kingdom by receiving Jesus, who is one of them, "gentle and humble of heart" (11:29).

Yahweh's Signet Ring

Haggai prophesied at a time when the Persian Empire was shaken from end to end with revolts, and it looked like it would collapse. "I will shake the heavens and the earth; I will overthrow the thrones of kingdoms. . . ." (Hg 2:21-22). When the Empire fell, Zerubbabel would be anointed king of a restored Israel! Or at least that is how Haggai seemed to understand God's words. "On that day, says the Lord of hosts, I will take you, Zerubbabel . . . and I will set you as a signet ring; for I have chosen you, says the Lord" (Hg 2:23, n). But Haggai saw only a small part of the glorious work Yahweh would do. He was right in saying that God would do something world-shaking. Haggai knew that God would act and that he would act through a son of David. That much was certain. But Haggai thought Zerubbabel was that son.

As Yahweh's signet ring, Zerubbabel is the one Yahweh will use to give effect to his decrees; he is the chosen instrument for carrying out the messianic promises. The promise to Zerubbabel reverses the punishment of his grandfather, rejected as God's instrument:

As I live, says the Lord, if you Coniah, son of Jehoiakim, king of Judah, are a signet ring on my right hand, I will snatch you from it. I will deliver you into the hands of those who seek your life, the hands of those whom you fear, the hands of Nebuchadnezzar, king of Babylon, and the Chaldeans. I will cast you out, you and the mother who bore you, into a different land from the one you were born in; and there you shall die (Jer 22:24-26, n).

Will Yahweh restore the throne of David to Coniah's grandson? Persia does not collapse, Darius masters all the revolts, the empire is restored to peace, the kingdom of David is not restored, Zerubbabel never comes to the throne. Was Haggai wrong?

Not at all. The truth he expressed as the word of the Lord was infinitely larger than he dreamed. God used Zerubbabel to restore hope by rebuilding the temple. This rebuilding was part of God's long-range preparation for the coming of the Messiah. Haggai was right when he said that God would act in a world-shaking way. The rebuilt temple would in some way prepare for this. Haggai aroused faith and hope in the messianic promises. When immediate expectations failed to materialize, it became clear that his words to Zerubbabel would be fulfilled in some future act of God. "My spirit continues in your midst!" (Hg 2:5, n).

When Matthew speaks of an earthquake that occurs as Jesus enters Jerusalem and the temple, he tells us what this future act of God is. He has already taken care to tell us that Jesus is descended from Zerubbabel, son of Shealtiel, son of Jechoniah (Coniah) (Mt 1:12). He shows Jesus coming as Messiah, Son of David, God's signet ring, to that temple which Zerubbabel had built and Herod had embellished (Mt 21:9, 12). The city is shaken as if by an earthquake as he enters. As he comes into the temple, the words of Haggai are fulfilled in a way undreamed of by the prophet: "I will shake all the nations, and the treasures of all the nations will come in . . . I will fill this house with glory" (Hg 2:7, n).

Influenced, no doubt, by Jesus' fulfillment of this verse, the Latin Vulgate had translated "treasures of the nations" as "desideratus gentibus"—the One desired by all the nations; Jesus, the One treasured by the nations! "Where your treasure is, there your heart is also" (Mt 6:21).

But Jesus' entrance into the temple symbolizes something

still greater. Matthew interprets this symbol by enclosing the whole chapter within references to Psalm 118. Jesus is the stone who is desecrated when he is rejected, but in his resurrection he is consecrated as the living temple (Mt 21:42). He is the house of prayer for all the nations.

"I will shake all the nations, and the treasures of all the nations will come in" (Hg 2:7, n). Obviously Haggai was thinking of more than material treasures being brought in as tribute to decorate the temple in glorious splendor: "I will fill my house with glory." He was thinking of people of all nations coming to worship in the temple and bringing their treasures as votive offerings. Isaiah, chapter 60, more or less contemporary with Haggai, expresses this idea in an elaborate, poetic way. It too is background for Matthew, chapter 21, and Matthew has already presented it as a backdrop for the story of the Magi. "They were overjoyed at seeing the star, and on entering *the house*, found the child with Mary, his mother. "They prostrated themselves and did him homage. Then they opened their coffers and presented him with gifts of gold, frankincense, and myrrh" (Mt 2:10-11). These words correspond with, "All from Sheba shall come bearing gold and frankincense, and proclaiming the praises of the Lord". . . . They will be acceptable offerings on my altar, and I will enhance the splendor of *my house*" (Is 60:6-7, n).

At the coming of the Magi, too, Jerusalem is deeply shaken. "King Herod became greatly disturbed, and with him all Jerusalem" (Mt 2:3, n). The earthshaking event of Jesus has begun, the treasures of the nations are already coming in. Jesus, the new temple, is the house of prayer for all the nations. The Magi represent the nations coming to worship and bringing their treasures to one greater than Solomon. All the nations shall "enter the house" (cf. Mt 2:11; Is 56:4-6).

And all this because the stone that the builders rejected has become the keystone of the structure. "By the Lord has this been done! It is wonderful in our eyes!" (Ps 118:23, n).

We acclaim the risen Lord in every Eucharistic celebration in the words of that same psalm: "Blessed is he who comes in the name of the Lord! Hosanna in the highest!"

FIFTEEN

Innocent Blood Betrayed

Judas "went out and hanged himself" (Mt 27:5, r). The section of the gospel containing these words is usually given the title, "The Death of Judas." But this suicide is not Matthew's main point. Judas' death is dismissed in five brief words. The real theme of this section is the pieces of silver, the price of blood. The silver pieces are mentioned seven times, four times as a noun and three times as a pronoun. The blood is mentioned three times.

> When Judas, his betrayer, saw that he was condemned, he repented and brought back the thirty pieces of silver to the chief priests and the elders, saying, "I have sinned in betraying innocent blood" (Mt 27:3-4, r).

Innocent blood is a theme or thread running all through Matthew's tapestry portrait of Jesus. We cannot grasp its full meaning unless we look at the earlier appearances of the thread.

The thread begins in the story of the Magi, where Herod murders the innocent infants of Bethlehem. Though the word "blood" is not mentioned in that story, Jesus will refer to the blood of these children when he speaks of the coming judgment upon all who have shed innocent blood:

> Woe to you, scribes and Pharisees, hypocrites! for you build the tombs of the prophets and adorn the monuments of

the righteous, saying, "If we had lived in the days of our fathers, we would not have taken part with them in shedding the blood of the prophets." Thus you witness against yourselves, that you are sons of those who murdered the prophets. Fill up, then, the measure of your fathers. You serpents, you brood of vipers, how are you to escape being sentenced to hell? Therefore I send you prophets and wise men and scribes, some of whom you will kill and crucify, and some you will scourge in your synagogues and persecute from town to town, that upon you may come *all the righteous blood* shed on earth, from the blood of innocent Abel to the blood of Zechariah, the son of Barachiah, whom you murdered between the sanctuary and the altar (Mt 23:29-35, r).

Abel and Zechariah are the first and last murdered persons mentioned in the Hebrew Bible, and thus they symbolize the first and last members of the human race to be murdered, and all those in between. The blood of the innocents of Bethlehem is connected with "all the righteous blood" through the reference to the wise men, "I send you prophets and wise men and scribes" (23:34). Just as wise men are sent to Herod, and the chief priests and the scribes of the people brought forth the witness of the prophets by quoting Micah to Herod (Mt 2:6), so Jesus will send prophets and wise men and scribes to his people after his resurrection. That is, he will send missionaries to them to call them to repentance for rejecting Jesus.

The Blood of Jesus

Matthew inserts the story of the thirty pieces of silver, the price of innocent blood, within the account of Jesus' trial before Pilate. First he shows how the assembled "chief priests and elders of the people took counsel" and brought Jesus before Pilate (Mt 27:1-2, r). But before he says another word about the trial, he presents the passage concerning the "blood money" (27:6). It is obvious that Judas' confrontation with the priests and elders did not take place during the trial, for he met them in the temple after he "saw that Jesus was condemned" (27:3). Why does Matthew insert this incident in the midst of the account of the trial?

In doing so, he powerfully dramatizes the unjustness of the trial. First, Judas, the betrayer, admits the injustice of all that is happening, saying, "I have sinned in betraying innocent blood" (27:4, r). And he throws down the price of his treachery. At first, the priests do not even want to listen to him. They say, "What is that to us? That is your concern." But they end by agreeing, for when they pick up the silver pieces thrown down by Judas, they say, "It is the price of blood." It is money tainted by sin, and therefore, according to a legal principle from the Law of Moses (Dt 23:18, r), it may not be put into the sacred temple treasury.

The very priests who tainted this money by buying innocent blood with it and desecrating the person of the Lord, worry about desecrating the temple treasury with blood money! How easily we deceive ourselves that we are holy even in the midst of our greatest crimes! Our concern for worship, or for other good causes, camouflages the dead bones within us. "You are like whitewashed tombs, which outwardly appear beautiful, but within they are full of dead men's bones and all uncleanness" (Mt 23:27, r). I think of a certain Chicago gangster, guilty of a number of gang murders, who gives a great dinner for the poor each Christmas, yet never stops his murderous activities. But do not all of us do this sort of thing on a smaller scale? For example, we justify the fornication or adultery that we commit by calling it "love." Or in a show of "righteous" zeal for God, we are severe with sinners.

"His Blood Be On Us"

The theme of innocent blood continues in the story of the trial before Pilate. Pilate refuses to take responsibility for the blood of Jesus. He says to the crowds, "I am innocent of this man's blood; see to it yourselves" (27:24, r). He is like the priests and elders, who said the same words to Judas, "See to it yourself!" (27:4, r).

But the crowds accept the responsibility. "All the people answered, 'His blood be on us and on our children!'" (27:25, r).

Without realizing it, the priests and elders, too, had admitted their responsibility for the blood of Jesus by admitting that the thirty silver pieces were blood money. Their refusal to put the tainted money into the temple treasury spoke loudly of their guilt. Their hearts recognized that this blood money had betrayed an innocent man. They betrayed their guilt by their act of seeming religious reverence. Sooner or later, even the unrepentant are forced to testify to the innocence of Jesus.

Since the tainted money must not taint the holy treasury, "they took counsel" to decide how to dispose of it. These counselors are so conscientious! Again and again Matthew shows them on the job. They "took counsel together in order to arrest Jesus by stealth and kill him" (26:4, r). "All the chief priests and elders of the people took counsel against Jesus to put him to death" (27:1). When his tomb was found empty after his resurrection, again the priests assembled the elders, and when they had "taken counsel" they bribed the guards of the tomb (28:12). "They took counsel" concerning the thirty pieces of silver, "and bought with them the potter's field, to bury strangers in. Therefore that field has been called the Field of Blood to this day" (Mt 27:7-8, r).

Thus they fulfilled the prophecy of Zechariah: And they weighed out as my wages thirty shekels of silver. Then the Lord said to me, "Cast it into the treasury"—the lordly price at which I was paid off by them. So I took the thirty shekels of silver and cast them into the treasury in the house of the Lord (Zec 11:12-13, r).

Matthew freely adapts these words of Zechariah to show how they are fulfilled in the purchase of the potter's field:

The words of the prophet Jeremiah were then fulfilled: "And they took the thirty silver pieces, the sum at which the Precious One was priced by children of Israel, and they gave them for the potter's field, just as the Lord directed me" (Mt 27:9-10, j).

"Just as the Lord directed me" corresponds to the words of Zechariah, "The Lord said to me, 'Cast it into the treasury.'" Thus Matthew insists that the betrayal of Jesus is in accord with God's will and design. The very price of the betrayal is foretold by the prophet. The silver pieces are disposed of in accordance with God's command. The same Lord who commanded Zechariah to throw his thirty pieces into the treasury was in total command of all that resulted from Judas' betrayal of Jesus: "They gave them for the potter's field, just as the Lord directed me" (Mt 27:10). The derisory price paid for the innocent blood of the Precious One in no way devalues that blood. It is the blood shed for the redemption of all mankind!

At the same time, God's judgment upon Judas, upon the priests and elders, and upon the whole land of Israel, is manifest in the incident of the potter's field purchased by the price of blood. This becomes clear by Matthew's reference to Jeremiah: "The words of the prophet Jeremiah were then fulfilled: 'And they took the thirty silver pieces . . . and they gave them for the potter's field'" (Mt 27:9).

The Potter's Field

But the words that Matthew quotes are not from Jeremiah at all. They are from Zechariah. Why does Matthew write "Jeremiah" instead of "Zechariah?" He wants us to interpret these events with the help of Jeremiah as well as Zechariah. What Jeremiah did and said in the vicinity of this potter's field is very much to the point. An ancient and probably authentic tradition locates the potter's field, purchased for the price of Jesus' blood, in the Valley of Hinnom, just outside the southern gates of Jerusalem. Matthew's original readers were probably vividly aware of that place, and the reference to Jeremiah and the mention of the potter's field would make them think of what Jeremiah had done in that valley (Jer 19).

The Lord tells Jeremiah to buy a potter's earthen vessel (19:1). The potter's shop was probably on the way to the valley, the source of the potter's clay. In the presence of the elders and priests, Jeremiah smashes the pot in a prophetic action pronouncing judgment upon Jerusalem and its leaders and people.

Why did God send the elders and priests with Jeremiah to this particular spot for this prophetic action? The place itself formed a dramatic part of the message. From ancient Canaanite times, the valley Ge-hinnom, had been the site of the worship of Moloch, possibly a god of the underworld. People burned their children in sacrifices to this horrible god. The place of sacrifice was called Topheth, which means "furnace of fire." Kings Ahaz and Manasseh of Judah had revived this ancient cult (2 Kgs 16:3; 21:6).

In the youthful days of Jeremiah, King Josiah abolished this cult once again, and desecrated Topheth. It seems that it became a rubbish heap of broken pottery and other refuse. That must be why the gate leading to this city dump was called "The Potsherd Gate" (Jer 19:2). The name of the valley, Ge-hinnom, became "Gehenna" in Greek. Gehenna and its "furnace of fire" became a symbol of hell.

Smashing the potter's jar in this place, Jeremiah pronounces judgment upon Jerusalem. "Thus says the Lord of hosts: So will I break this people and this city, as one breaks a potter's vessel, so that it can never be mended. Men shall bury in Topheth the desecrated ground because there will be no place else to bury," so numerous will the corpses be! (Jer 19:10-12, r). "Therefore, behold, the days are coming, says the Lord, when it will no more be called Topheth, or the valley of the son of Hinnom, but the valley of Slaughter: for they will bury in Topheth, because there is no room elsewhere" (Jer 7:32-33, r). How tragic to be buried in desecrated ground!

When Matthew says that the purchase of the potter's field fulfilled the words of Jeremiah, he wants us to think first of all of what Jeremiah did in that valley where the field is located. There the prophet smashed the potter's vessel to dramatize God's judgment upon the people of Jerusalem and its leaders. Thus

Matthew shows that he regards the death of Judas as a divine judgment. Judas's own words, "I have sinned in betraying innocent blood," echo the reason given by Jeremiah for the judgment upon Jerusalem in his day: "The kings of Judah . . . have filled this place with the blood of the innocents" (Jer 19:4, r).

The judgment upon Judas foreshadows the coming judgment upon Jerusalem. Jerusalem has shed the innocent blood of Jesus, bringing to a last full measure all the innocent blood shed since the beginning of time. "Now it is your turn: Fill up the vessel measured out by your forefathers. Viper's nest! Brood of serpents! How can you escape condemnation to Gehenna? . . . O Jerusalem, Jerusalem, murderess of prophets and stoner of those who are sent to you!" (Mt 23:32-37, n). Our Lord's reference here to Gehenna should have stirred memories of Jeremiah's action in smashing the pottery in the Valley of Gehenna. Once again the valley will be a burial place, and not just for a few foreigners in the potter's field!

The Precious One

After referring us to Jeremiah and his judgment prophecy in the Valley of Gehenna, Matthew goes on to quote Zechariah's passage about thirty pieces of silver. Thus he points this message of judgment directly at the rulers of Judah, who have purchased Jesus, their God, for thirty silver pieces: "The words of Jeremiah were then fulfilled. 'And they took the thirty silver pieces, the sum at which the Precious One was priced by the children of Israel, and they gave them for the potter's field, just as the Lord directed me'" (Mt 27:9-10, j).

The Precious One in Matthew is, of course, Jesus. But in Zechariah the Precious One is God himself (Zec 11:4-17). Zechariah's passage is an allegory in which the prophet becomes shepherd of God's flock. The flock is the people who are exploited by their greedy rulers: "Thus said the Lord my God: Shepherd the flock to be slaughtered. For they who buy them slay them with impunity; while those who sell them say, 'Blessed be the Lord, I have become rich!' Even their own shepherds do not feel for them" (Zec 11:4-5, n).

The rulers who buy and sell the people praise God for their own enrichment! Here again we have a show of religion camouflaging wickedness. "So I became the shepherd of the flock to be slaughtered for the sheep merchants. . . . I said to them, 'If it seems good to you, give me my wages; but if not, let it go.' And they counted out my wages, thirty pieces of silver" (Zec 11:7, 12, n).

The services of this good shepherd are contemptuously valued at thirty silver pieces, the legal indemnity for a gored slave (Ex 21:32). "But the Lord said to me, 'Throw it in the treasury, the handsome price at which they valued me.' So I took the thirty pieces of silver and threw them into the treasury in the house of the Lord" (Zec 11:13, n).

Thrown into the temple treasury, the money is paid to God. Since the prophet is God's personal representative in shepherding God's flock, these children of Israel are despising God himself in valuing the prophet at the price of a slave. How shamefully they repay God's love and care!

Zechariah, whose services are valued at thirty silver pieces, is a type (a prefigurement) of Jesus, whose mission of salvation to his people was appraised by the Sanhedrists, the false shepherds, at the same base price, about $120.00.

We find varying translations of Zechariah's words. "Then the Lord said to me: Throw it to the *potter*—the magnificent value at which I was valued by them" (Zec 11:13, m). "Then the Lord said to me: Cast it into the *treasury*—the lordly price at which I was paid off by them" (r). The reason for this is that these variations exist in the ancient manuscripts. Some scholars explain that the man who melted down the metals offered to the treasury happened to be a potter. Before long, the word "potter" became the word for "treasurer." If that is so, then Zechariah did give the money to the treasury.

This happy circumstance that associates potter and treasury served Matthew's purposes very well. He shows the plan of God at work when the money that must not taint the sacred treasury is used to purchase a potter's field. God is in command of everything. He brings good even out of Judas' treachery and his desecration of the innocent blood of the Precious One.

Matthew freely adapts the words of Zechariah, changing "I" to "They." Zechariah says, "*I* took the thirty pieces of silver and threw them into the treasury in the house of the Lord." Matthew, adapting these words to the priests and elders, says, "*They* took the thirty silver pieces . . . and gave them for the potter's field, just as the Lord directed *me*." Matthew retains the last phrase in the first person, "just as the Lord directed me," referring it back to Zechariah who said, "Then the Lord said to me." The Lord directed Zechariah to put his wages into the treasury. Matthew, using "they," to speak of the priests buying the potter's field, ends by saying, "just as the Lord directed *me*." Thus he shifts our attention back from the priests to Zechariah, the shepherd who prefigures the purchased Jesus. Thus Zechariah's words seem to ring forth from the lips of Jesus: "Throw it into the treasury, the handsome price at which they valued me!"

Judgment comes upon the priests and elders who have bought their Lord at this insulting price. The judgment upon Judas who sold him warns of the judgment coming upon those who bought him. The potter's field Akeldama, the Field of Blood, acts as a standing witness against those false shepherds, the Sanhedrists, who should have shepherded Israel instead of being sheep merchants ready to slaughter the flock.

They become symbols of many of our contemporary world rulers who use their positions more for their own power and profit than for the good of the people they govern. They will come under God's judgment, like the leaders of the people in Zechariah's allegory, who are called "sheep merchants" instead of "shepherds," because they buy sheep and slay them without a qualm of conscience, just as the priests and elders bought and killed Jesus. Therefore the oppressed people are called "the flock to be slaughtered."

We can hear God's words to Zechariah as though they are addressed to Jesus: "Thus says the Lord, my God: Shepherd the flock to be slaughtered." And we hear Jesus' response: "So I became the shepherd of the flock to be slaughtered for the sheep merchants" (Zec 11:4, 7, n).

Those people of Jerusalem who approved of the death of

Jesus, plotted by their leaders, do indeed become "the flock to be slaughtered" along with "the sheep merchants" when the Romans destroy their city in 70 A.D. They reject the missionaries sent to them by the risen Lord (Mt 23:34), and therefore "retribution overtakes you for all the blood of the just ones shed on earth" (Mt 23:35, n).

Judas had been called as a shepherd in the messianic community. But he betrayed his call, just as those shepherds of Israel who purchased Jesus betrayed theirs. Judas' treachery reminds us that shepherds in the church established by Jesus are capable of treachery, just as were the shepherds of the Old Law. The priests and elders who condemned Jesus stand as a warning for bishops and priests today.

The Blood Comes into God's Presence

"Throw it into the treasury, the handsome price at which they valued me!" (Zec 11:13, n). Matthew tells us that Judas threw his thirty pieces, not into the treasury, but into the *naos*, the sanctuary (the holy of holies).

The *naos* was the place of the Divine Presence. No one was permitted to enter into this Presence except the high priest. And he entered only once a year, on the Day of Atonement, carrying the blood of a sacrifice which he offered for himself and for the sins of the people (Heb 9:7; Lv 16:1-19).

Thus, when Judas throws his silver pieces towards the sanctuary, the price of the blood of Jesus is cast as it were into the very presence of God, just as on the Day of Atonement the blood of the atoning sacrifice was carried into that holy place. We think of the words of Hebrews:

But when Christ came as high priest of the good things which have come to be, he entered once for all into the sanctuary, passing through the greater and more perfect tabernacle not made by hands, that is, not belonging to this creation. He entered, not with the blood of goats and calves, but with his own blood, and achieved eternal redemption (Heb 9:11-12, n).

Thus the horrible crime of selling innocent blood is turned into a blessing. The blood of the Precious One wins our salvation.

Judas Judged

The Acts of the Apostles gives us a different version of the potter's field story (Acts 1:15-20). According to Acts, Judas did not throw the money into the holy place, nor into the temple treasury, but used it to buy the field himself. While working on the field, it seems, he fell, perhaps upon a sharp rock, and broke open.

Which tradition was closer to the facts as they actually happened? It doesn't really matter. The important point made by the inspired scriptures is the divine meaning of these events. If Acts is factual, Matthew's version may well have been a midrash, a retelling of the story to bring out the spiritual meaning, pointing out that Judas' death was a judgment of God. Just as Topheth, under God's judgment, became the burial place of a massacred people, so the field that Judas bought became a burial place for foreigners. But the innocent blood that purchased the field came into the presence of God, into the heavenly *naos*, for the salvation of the nations.

Like Matthew, Acts has its midrashic elements. The story of Akeldama, the Field of Blood, is interpreted with the help of some verses from the psalms. Peter applies the words, "Let another take his office" (Ps 109:8, r) to the apostolic ministry to which Judas had been called. Judas was "numbered among us, and was allotted his share in this ministry" (Acts 1:17, r).

In the Old Law, priests and Levites owned no land. No fields were allotted to them when the promised land was divided among the tribes. God himself was the apportioned lot of the tribe of Levi. They were to minister to God in his presence: "O Lord, my allotted portion and my cup, you it is who hold fast my lot. For me the measuring lines have fallen on pleasant sites; fair to me indeed is my inheritance" (Ps 16:5-6, n).

Judas was allotted his share in the ministry of the apostles (1:17). But he sold this fair inheritance for a piece of land and forfeited his companionship with the Lord for a field of blood.

Peter points out another psalm also fulfilled in Judas: "May their camp be a desolation, let no one dwell in their tents" (Ps 69:25, r). Peter restates this to apply to Judas: "Let his habitation become desolate, and let there be no one to live in it" (Acts 1:20, r).

The desolation of the field of blood after the violent death of its owner symbolizes the desolation of Israel when God leaves the temple: "You will find your temple deserted" (Mt 23:38, n).

SIXTEEN

The Potter's Field:
Symbol of Hope

Then was fulfilled what had been spoken by the prophet Jeremiah, saying, "And they took the thirty pieces of silver, the price of him on whom a price had been set by some of the sons of Israel, and they gave them for the potter's field, as the Lord directed me (Mt 27:9-10, r).

Secured at the price of the Lord's blood, the potter's field is a symbol of hope, both for Israel and for all the nations. The note of salvation sounds in all eleven fulfillment texts in Matthew. This too, therefore, must be a salvation passage.

The note of salvation is sounded in this passage first in a general way, since salvation comes to mankind precisely because the blood of Jesus was despised and sold for thirty silver pieces. But Matthew probably has something even more specific in mind. Though he quotes here only words from Zechariah, he says that the buying of the potter's field fulfills the words of Jeremiah. Jeremiah, too, bought a field for silver (Jer 32:10) and buried the deed of purchase in a potter's jar (Jer 32:14).

Jeremiah's purchase of this field was a sign of hope for the people of Jerusalem and Judah who were about to be expelled from their fields and vineyards and driven off to exile in Babylon:

In their presence I gave Baruch this charge: Thus says the Lord of hosts, the God of Israel: Take these deeds, both the

143

sealed and the open deed of purchase, and put them in an earthen jar, so that they can be kept there a long time. For thus says the Lord of hosts, the God of Israel: Houses and fields and vineyards shall again be bought in this land (Jer 32:13-15, n).

Immediately after giving the deed of purchase to Baruch, Jeremiah prays to the Lord concerning the land of Israel and the piece of it that he himself has just purchased:

Ah, Lord God, you have made heaven and earth by your great might, with your outstretched arm; nothing is impossible to you. . . . With hand and outstretched arm you brought your people Israel out of the lands of Egypt. . . . This land you gave them, as you had promised their fathers under oath, a land flowing with milk and honey. They entered and took possession of it, but they did not listen to your voice. . . . Hence you let all these evils befall them. See, the siegeworks have arrived at this city to breach it; the city will be handed over to the Chaldeans who are attacking it, amid sword, famine, and pestilence. What you threatened has happened, you see it yourself. And yet you tell me, O Lord God: Buy the field with money, call in witnesses. But the city has already been handed over to the Chaldeans! (Jer 32:17, 21-25, n).

The Lord responds to this prayer, admitting all these evils, and even referring again to the Valley of Ben-hinnom and the sacrifice of children to Moloch in the furnace of fire. Yet in spite of these abominations, the Lord speaks a word of great hope:

I am the Lord, the God of all mankind! Is anything impossible to me? . . . Concerning this city, which as you say is handed over to the king of Babylon amid sword, famine, and pestilence: Behold, I will gather them together from all the lands to which in anger, wrath and great rage I banish them; I will bring them back to this place and settle them here in safety. . . . One heart and one way I will give them. . . . I will make with them an eternal covenant, never to cease doing good to them. . . . Fields shall again be bought in this land. . . . Fields shall be bought with money, deeds written and sealed, and witnesses shall be used . . . when I change their lot, says the Lord (Jer 32:27, 36-37, 39-40, 43-44, n).

This message of hope is echoed in the words of Matthew: "What was said through Jeremiah the prophet was fulfilled: 'They took the thirty pieces of silver . . . and they paid it out for the potter's field, just as the Lord had commanded me'" (Mt 27:9-10, n).

Just as Zechariah, by the Lord's command, threw his silver pieces into the treasury, so by command of the Lord Jeremiah bought his field:

This message came to me from the Lord, said Jeremiah: Hanamel, son of your uncle Shallum, will come to you with the offer: "Buy for yourself my field in Anathoth, since you, as nearest relative, have the first right of purchase." Then, as the Lord foretold, Hanamel, my uncle's son, came to me to the quarters of the guard and said, "Please buy my field in Anathoth, in the district of Benjamin; as nearest relative, you have the first claim to possess it; make it yours." I knew this was what the Lord meant, so I bought the field from my cousin Hanamel, paying him the money, seventeen silver shekels (Jer 32:6-9, n).

Jeremiah bought that particular field at the Lord's command precisely because he was *go'el*, nearest relative, with the responsibility of redeeming the field lest it be alienated from the family. "For the right of redemption by purchase is yours" (Jer 32:6, r). In ancient Israel, whenever a person got himself into difficulties, his next of kin had the responsibility of redeeming him from his troubles. If, for example, he had to be sold into slavery to pay off his debts, his closest blood relative had to redeem him. Or if his patrimony had to be sold, his next of kin had the right to buy it, lest it pass out of the clan. This was the case when Jeremiah bought that field. The Hebrew word for the next of kin was *go'el*, and the word also meant "redeemer." That is how it is translated each time that God calls himself Israel's *go'el*. By reason of his blood covenant with her, God is Israel's blood relative, her next of kin, her redeemer.

Jeremiah as *go'el* redeems his cousin's field, purchasing it for silver pieces. Jesus, redeemer of his people, purchases back Israel's heritage for her at the price of his own blood, which she appraised at thirty pieces of silver!

The Lord's blood was a price not paid in vain! The whole account of "the Field of Blood" carries a message of hope. It is not far-fetched to interpret Matthew's account in this way. Matthew was an expert at midrash, a Jewish manner of re-telling the scriptures so that they would fit new situations, in order to bring out the divine meaning of these events. It was a technique for making scriptures relevant to life.

It is sometimes suggested that Matthew merely made a mistake when he attributed Zechariah's words to Jeremiah. But Matthew shows such amazing knowledge of scriptures that he could hardly make a mistake like that. It is more likely that he is simply dropping a midrashic clue. He is sending us back to Jeremiah by his words refering to the purchase of a piece of land.

Others Reap the Harvest

Jeremiah bought that piece of land precisely to keep it in the family. But Israel lost its land when the keepers of the vineyard killed the owner's son: "When they saw the son, the tenants said to one another, 'Here is the one who will inherit everything. Let us kill him and then we shall have his inheritance!' With that they seized him, dragged him outside the vineyard, and killed him" (Mt 21:37-38, n).

For this reason, Israel lost its inheritance, the land God had given to their forefathers. Or more exactly, they lost the kingdom of God, the inheritance that God had promised them: "For this reason, I tell you, the kingdom of God will be taken away from you and given to a nation that will yield a rich harvest" (Mt 21:43, n).

By saying, "Let his blood be on us and on our children" (Mt 27:25, n), some of the people ratified the decision of their leaders to kill Jesus. Thus they lost their fruitful vineyard and, like Judas, had only a "field of blood," a potter's field, as their patrimony. Others will reap the harvest they should have had.

The thread of thought which began when the land drank in the blood of innocent Abel surfaces again in Matthew's account of the Field of Blood (Mt 27:8). Jesus himself points to this thread when he says to those who reject him, "Fill up, then, the measure of your fathers . . . that upon you may come all the righteous blood shed on earth, from the blood of innocent Abel to the blood of Zechariah. . . ." (Mt 23:32, 35, r).

There will be an accounting for all this blood, including all the innocent blood that is flowing so freely in the twentieth century. Thousands of innocent children may have been sacrificed to Moloch in the furnace of fire in the Valley of Hinnom, but millions of them are murdered each year in America's abortion clinics.

When Jesus mentions "the blood of innocent Abel," words from Genesis at once begin to echo in our hearts:

The Lord then said: "What have you done! Listen: Your brother's blood cries out to me from the soil! Therefore you shall be banned from the soil that opened its mouth to receive your brother's blood from your hand. If you till the soil, it shall no longer give you its produce. You shall become a restless wanderer on the earth" (Gn 4:10-12, n).

Thus Cain too had a "field of blood" as his patrimony. He is expelled from the fields that drank in his brother's blood. They no longer give him a harvest. Cain prefigures the keepers of the vineyard who lost their land when they shed the blood of Jesus, and others reaped the harvest that would have been theirs (Mt 21:43). The sterile fig tree cursed by Jesus symbolizes the sterility of the land that has drunk in the Savior's blood, and the judgment that is pronounced upon those who reject the Savior (Mt 21:18-22).

The judgment of God is manifest first of all in Judas, who

does not profit from his infamous gain. The priests and elders buy a piece of land with money they themselves admit is tainted by their commerce with Judas. Thus they inscribe the testimony of their crime on the very land, which is stigmatized "even to this day" by the name "Field of Blood" (Mt 27:8, c).

In reality, that name belongs not just to Israel's land. It belongs to all the earth. The soil drank in the blood of innocent Abel. Mankind continues to shed innocent blood freely all over our greedy and warring globe, and the whole earth is a field of blood. The earth is redeemed by the innocent Blood of Jesus. "The Field of Blood" is a sign of hope, not just for Israel, but for the whole human race.

Is that perhaps the divine significance of "the potter's field *to bury strangers*" (Mt 27:7, r). Foreigners, not Israelites, are buried in the land that drank the innocent blood of Jesus. "Through baptism into his death *we were buried with him*, so that, just as Christ was raised from the dead by the glory of the Father, we too might live a new life" (Rm 6:4, n).

The Blood Poured Out for "the Many"

"Take this and eat it," he said, "this is my body." Then he took a cup, gave thanks, and gave it to them. "All of you must drink from it," he said, "for this is my blood, the blood of the covenant, to be poured out in behalf of *many* for the forgiveness of sins" (Mt 26:26-28, n).

"The many," we said earlier, signifies all mankind. Jesus poured out his blood for all those upon whom the Father pours out the rain and the sunshine. But now, without contradicting this, we can say that "the many" signifies the community of Israel, the people of the covenant of Sinai.

According to the Anchor Bible, the expression "the many" (*harabbim*) had a definite meaning for the Jewish people. This is clear from the Talmudic literature, the writings of the rabbis. *Harabbim*, "the many," consistently meant the covenant people, the covenant community of Israel. For this reason, in the Anchor Bible we read: The Son of Man "did not come to be served, but to serve, and to give his life as a ransom *for the community*" the many (Mt 20:28, a). Jesus applies to himself Isaiah's words concerning the Suffering Servant, who gives his life as a ransom for the covenant people: "If he gives his life as an offering for sin . . . by his knowledge shall the righteous one, my servant, make many *harabbim* to be accounted righteous" (Is 53:10, n; 53:11, r).

The prophet describes the servant as an innocent man who rescues his fellow Israelites from suffering by bearing their sufferings himself. "Surely he has borne our griefs and carried our sorrows" (Is 53:4, r). The servant, the righteous one, will bring righteousness to the community of Israel which has so misunderstood him. "He was despised and rejected by men . . . and we esteemed him not" (53:3, r).

Matthew's thesis is that Jesus came to fulfill the law and the prophets and so fulfill all righteousness, and to call Israel back to covenant love, the very essence of the law and the prophets. It is quite likely that the Anchor Bible rightly translates the words of Jesus: "The Son of Man did not come to be served, but to *serve*, and to give his life as a ransom *for the community*" of Israel.

Certainly this is St. Paul's thesis. "For I tell you that Christ became a *servant* to the circumcised to show God's truthfulness, in order to confirm the promises given to the patriarchs" (Rm 15:8, r). Jesus gives his life precisely as servant to the circumcised, the covenant people of Israel. Therefore, in Matthew, Jesus preaches only to the covenant people: "My mission is only to the lost sheep of the house of Israel" (Mt 15:24, n).

Jesus voluntarily pours out his life for the community of Israel, and, in so doing, inaugurates a new covenant for the covenant community that already exists. To be saved, the rest of mankind must be incorporated into the community, which is heir to and continuous with the Israel of the old covenant, the messianic community redeemed by the blood of Jesus.

In its fulfillment by Jesus, the covenant with Israel is extended to all mankind. The blood of Jesus given for the people of the covenant, "the many," is given for all mankind, for all peoples are called into Israel's covenant, which comes to full maturity in the messianic community gathered together in the blood of Jesus.

For it was God's eternal plan to save mankind through the people of Israel. "Salvation is from the Jews," says Jesus (Jn 4:22, n). "In your descendants all the nations of the earth shall find blessing," said God to Abraham (Gn 22:18, n).

Those who have rejected Jesus, whether Gentiles or Jews, have a standing invitation to come back to him, to enter into the new and eternal covenant he has made with the Israel of old in his own blood, the covenant into which the Gentiles, too, have been called.

As he leaves the temple, Jesus warns, "Recall the saying, 'You will find your temple deserted'" (Mt 23:38, n). But then he adds words of hope, promising that he will come to all who turn to him in repentence: "I tell you, you will not see me from this time on until you declare, 'Blessed is he who comes in the name of the Lord'" (Mt 23:39, n).

We acclaim him *now*, saying, "Hosanna to the Son of David! Blessed is he who comes in the name of the Lord! Hosanna in the highest!" (Mt 21:9).

We repeat these words daily in the Eucharistic Liturgy, when we celebrate the new and eternal covenant in the blood which was shed for the many, the community of God's people which has become the Eucharistic community. "Blessed is he who comes in the name of the Lord! Hosanna in the highest!"